Freeform Style

Freeform *Style*

Blend Knit *and* Crochet *to* Create Fiber Art Wearables

Prudence Mapstone and Jonelle Raffino

NORTH LIGHT BOOKS
Cincinnati, Ohio

www.mycraftivity.com

Freeform Style. Copyright © 2009 by Prudence Mapstone and Jonelle Raffino. Manufactured in China. All rights reserved. The patterns and drawings in the book are for personal use of reader. By permission of the author and publisher, they may be either hand-traced or photocopied to make single copies, but under no circumstances may they be resold or republished. It is permissible for the purchaser to make the projects contained herein and sell them at fairs, bazaars and craft shows. No other part of this book may be reproduced in any form or by any electronic or mechanical means including information storage and retrieval systems without permission in writing from the publisher, except by a reviewer, who may quote a brief passage in review. Published by North Light Books, an imprint of F+W Media, Inc., 4700 East Galbraith Road, Cincinnati, Ohio 45236. (800) 289-0963.
First edition.

13 12 11 10 09   5 4 3 2 1

Distributed in Canada by Fraser Direct
100 Armstrong Avenue
Georgetown, ON, Canada L7G 5S4
Tel: (905) 877-4411

Distributed in the U.K. and Europe by David & Charles
Brunel House, Newton Abbot, Devon, TQ12 4PU, England
Tel: (+44) 1626 323200, Fax: (+44) 1626 323319
E-mail: postmaster@davidandcharles.co.uk

Distributed in Australia by Capricorn Link
P.O. Box 704, S. Windsor, NSW 2756 Australia
Tel: (02) 4577-3555

Library of Congress Cataloging-in-Publication Data
Mapstone, Prudence.
  Freeform style : blend knit and crochet to create fiber art wearables / Prudence Mapstone and Jonelle Raffino.
     p. cm.
  Includes index.
  ISBN 978-1-60061-138-4 (pbk. w/ flaps : alk. paper)
  1. Knitting--Patterns. 2. Crocheting--Patterns. I. Raffino, Jonelle. II. Title.
  TT825.M25 2009
  746.43'0432--dc22
                              2008042969

Metric Conversion Chart

to convert	to	multiply by
Inches	Centimeters	2.54
Centimeters	Inches	0.4
Feet	Centimeters	30.5
Centimeters	Feet	0.03
Yards	Meters	0.9
Meters	Yards	1.1
Sq. Inches	Sq. Centimeters	6.45
Sq. Centimeters	Sq. Inches	0.16
Sq. Feet	Sq. Meters	0.09
Sq. Meters	Sq. Feet	10.8
Sq. Yards	Sq. Meters	0.8
Sq. Meters	Sq. Yards	1.2
Pounds	Kilograms	0.45
Kilograms	Pounds	2.2
Ounces	Grams	28.3
Grams	Ounces	0.035

EDITORS
Liz Casler, Jessica Gordon and Robin M. Hampton

DESIGNER
Geoff Raker

PRODUCTION COORDINATOR
Greg Nock

PHOTOGRAPHERS
Ric Deliantoni, Al Parrish and Christine Polomsky

WARDROBE STYLIST
Monica Skrzelowski

PHOTO STYLIST
Lauren Emmerling

MAKEUP ARTIST
Cass Brake

TECHNICAL EDITOR
Amy Polcyn

fw
media
www.fwmedia.com

Dedication

We take great pride in the international community of friends we have made through our freeform art. The freeform group on Yahoo! continues to be a place where we find inspiration, guidance and the most wonderful group of creative women. Many members of that group contributed to the scarf showcase here and to other projects we have done. *Freeform Style* is dedicated to these ladies who we proudly call our friends, mentors and freeform family.

Acknowledgments

FROM JONELLE: I first fell in love with freeform many years ago when I stumbled upon some of Prudence's early work. I was captivated by the complexity of the colors and textures. Even with twenty years of knitting experience, I could not imagine being that good or creating such amazing things.

When I finally met Prudence and had the privilege of taking her workshops, I knew that my knitting and crochet would never be the same. My grandmothers taught me to follow a pattern like it was the law. A weekend of freeform unraveled the entire notion of a pattern. It challenged the way I knit, crocheted and designed. Learning freeform opened my eyes and made me an artist. It was a truly powerful learning experience.

Today I look back and realize that the process of learning to freeform expanded my power as a fiber artist and designer. I have learned to take simple garments and give them a freeform embellishment that makes them memorable. When I see a pattern I like, freeform allows me to give it my own special touch. More importantly, I have never had a scrap of yarn that could not be freeformed into something.

Prudence Mapstone has been one of the most influential artists in my career. She is my mentor and has inspired my journey as an artist. The projects in this book reflect the techniques and artwork that she has created in her years of teaching freeform around the world. It is my honor to coauthor *Freeform Style* with her, but I bow to her talent. She has made my yarns, the yarns of SWTC Inc., beautiful with her amazing work.

FROM PRUDENCE: Jonelle Raffino is President of South West Trading Company, one of the pioneers in the manufacture of earth friendly yarns. A family company, SWTC was the first to introduce SOYSILK® brand fiber (made from the residue of soybeans used in the creation of tofu) to spinners, then soon after they produced a SOYSILK® hand knitting yarn. A few years later they introduced to the U.S. market some of the first yarns made from bamboo…and not long after that developed a 100 percent corn fiber yarn.

As Jonelle has noted, we first met when she booked in to do a number of workshops I was conducting…and I have to report that I have hardly ever met a more enthusiastic or willing student! It is always thrilling for a tutor when a student gets excited about the methods you are demonstrating, but as a freeformer it is even better to watch someone immediately take off in their own direction, the ideas coming thick and fast. The only downside is that, unfortunately, their hooks and needles can't possibly keep up! I think she had most definitely found her creative niche at those workshops, and I'm sure she didn't sleep much during those first few freeforming days, but each morning she was back bright and early with additional swatches, new questions…and lots more yarn.

As the world looks toward more sustainable and environmentally friendly products, I think we can all look forward to seeing what other new and exciting yarns Jonelle and the SWTC team develop in the future.

Contents

Introduction

We love freeform because it has no rules. Errors become artistic enhancements, and color collides in a collage of yarns. Freeform can be wild and colorful or simple and elegant. It has no pattern and no boundaries: Anything you dream is possible.

Freeform combines several of our favorite fiber arts techniques, including knitting, crochet and even embroidery. It can be whatever you want it to be, from an easy embellishment that complements a garment to the entire fabric of the garment itself. Freeform can be a simple flat fabric or a 3-D masterpiece. In a freeform piece, knitting and crochet combine seamlessly to create a rich fabric that defies categorization. It is truly a medium that allows you to make things up as you go along.

Although freeform can look complex and maybe a bit intimidating, our primary goal for this book is to show you how simple it actually is. Too often we see even the most accomplished knitters and crocheters panic at the thought of trying freeform because it seems scary to do away with a pattern and work completely without a net. That's why, in this book, we give you the patterns in three levels, starting with a basic knit or crochet pattern that can be easily embellished with freeform techniques. In the next two levels, we slowly up the ante, encouraging you to incorporate more techniques and more colors. Once you feel comfortable with freeform, you can take off on your own creative journey, exploring stitches, color and texture. Our instructions are meant only as a guide. If you want to add more—just do it! Remember—there are no set rules! Push the boundaries.

If you fall in love with a stitch in one project, add it to the next—you have our permission! In fact, to us, it's a compliment. Not following the directions is a sign of success in freeform. Go with your instincts and allow yourself to break all of the rules you think you know about knitting and crochet.

Once you catch the freeform bug, you'll find that you set aside patterns and follow your own creative prowess. Open yourself to the possibilities that come when you try new yarns and new stitches, and repeatedly ask yourself, "Why not try it this way?" From the basic techniques, new strategies will develop. You'll discover an exciting new approach to your creative pursuits—the world we know as freeform.

— Prudence and Jonelle

Skill Levels

This book features patterns for ten different garments and accessories, each given at three different skill levels. Following is a description of the skills each level requires.

Level 1: For your first few freeform projects, we present our introduction to freeform in the form of the Level 1 patterns. Each of these projects begins with simple knit and crochet garments that can be embellished with just one or two freeform applications. We will introduce either knit or crochet techniques at this level, depending on the project. We'll talk you through basic methods and concepts so you can see how easy freeform is!

Level 2: You've already got the hang of freeform, and you are ready to take your art to the next level. So give these intermediate-level projects a try. Join us as we explore the use of several new stitches, combining texture and technique to give your project a more complex look and feel.

Level 3: There are no rules or patterns for advanced freeform. Call it the "Unpattern." Freeform unleashes the artist in each of us. Here we offer suggestions, tips and solutions, perhaps…but there are no rules. We hope the colors and textures of our collection will inspire you to create your own unique garments from here.

Materials and Tools

The great thing about freeform knit and crochet is that you can often make whatever you have on hand work for you! You may wish to use the tools and yarns you have while you are learning. If we recommend a G hook for the freeform embellishment and your H hook looks good…try it! With a bit of practice, you'll soon have confidence and experience. Then invest in the best yarns you can afford and make the project of your dreams.

Yarn

All of the projects in *Freeform Style* have been created with yarns from SWTC Inc., a company that pioneered the manufacture of earth-friendly yarns for hand knitting. In these projects, you will use bamboo, Soysilk®, milk fiber and even fiber from corn. The yarns are luxurious to work with and come in a fantastic array of colors that are well suited to multishade projects. The colors go together well within a specific yarn range and often across the entire SWTC collection. This allows you as an artist to combine several different yarns in one project with continuity and eye-catching elegance. Make sure to check out www.soysilk.com to see all the yarns and colors available. These yarns are sold at boutique yarn stores worldwide and through e-tailers as well. We encourage you to support your local yarn stores. These fine merchants are always there to answer questions and guide you in your fiber arts endeavors.

While freeform elements just beg for yarn substitution, the base patterns in *Freeform Style* were carefully created with the distinct properties of a particular yarn in mind. When substitutions are used, the results can be unpredictable. As with any project, if you decide to substitute a yarn from your stash, check your gauge carefully and always use a yarn similar in drape and feel.

Our favorite thing about freeform is that all of those wonderful bits in your stash can be incorporated into small details in your projects. A few yards of yarn from your stash might be fabulous for surface detail when making one of the vests in this book, or as a flower on your bamboo purse. Be careful not to add too many colors and textures, though! By nature, freeform can be enough excitement for one garment. Too many additional colors and textures can detract from the simple elegance of the pieces you admire most.

Crochet Hooks

Crochet hooks come in many sizes. Steel crochet hooks range in diameter from 0.4mm to 3.5mm (00 to 16 in American sizing). These hooks are used for fine crochet work. Aluminum, bamboo and plastic crochet hooks are available from 2.5mm to 19mm, or from B to S in American sizing. Our favorites are the hooks made by artists around the world. Many are hand carved in various woods. The most ornate are decorated with semiprecious stones or beads.

When selecting a hook for freeform, we have recommended a size for each product, but remember, there are no rules—try several sizes to see how your finished piece changes and decide which you like best. Sometimes choosing a size up or down can make the outcome unexpectedly and enjoyably different.

Knitting Needles

Knitting needles are as diverse as crochet hooks. Let your personal style and preferences guide your choice here. Experiment to see how different stitches, yarns and techniques look when worked with a variety of needle sizes.

Knitting needles come in common sizes ranging from US size 1 to 19 (2.25mm to 15.00mm). Larger sizes can be found in specialty stores. Your choice of straight, circular or double-pointed needles will depend on the project and your personal preference. In each project, we have noted our personal choice, but we invite you to experiment with other options.

Notions

There are a few other tools we recommend for your project bag. Scissors, a darning needle and a tape measure will come in handy. And stitch markers are a must-have for some of the larger projects.

Elements of Freeform

Freeform is simply the art of combining many different stitches and techniques into one beautiful fabric. In *Freeform Style*, we'll take something plain, such as the scarves in our first project, and by adding crochet discs and ovals and experimenting with a fun way to use I-cords, we'll make an otherwise fairly ordinary scarf amazing. Freeform will give it a whole new life. Check out some of the other garments, such as the bamboo vests on page 52. With some freeform magic, color, and some great new stitches, straightforward patterns can become works of art.

When you are done reading and experimenting with *Freeform Style*, these elements will become part of your artistic repertoire. Use your favorite techniques to jazz up everything you make. Find some of your old favorite plain garments and give them a whole new life.

Embellishments

Let's take our first look at some of the different embellishments we'll introduce in *Freeform Style*. These techniques can be used individually or in tandem. Most freeform starts with little patches that become the building blocks for the rest of your projects. However, thinking outside the box, Prudence tried something a little different this time, and applied the patches to the base garment as an artistic embellishment in their own right. As you practice this style of adornment, consider how you might also be able to use any of the ideas a little differently. Let your previous artistic experience and expertise inspire you! Always ask, "What if…?" We consider that a compliment!

Straight-Edged Patches

Small sections of knitting and crochet can be joined together and added to any garment to give it your personal touch. Arrange and sew the pieces straight onto the surface of the garment, or stitch them together first. Perhaps add some additional interest by working crochet stitches onto some of the knitting, as the mood takes you. Either keep every element similar for continuity (for example, all rectangular pieces), or throw in a few surprises (such as the crochet circles added to the knitting on page 17) for an even more unusual design.

Embroidery

Adding a few basic embroidery stitches here and there is a good way to help blend all of the various elements together. Even simple, straight stitches, such as those worked in clusters in the photo on page 16, will lend a certain cohesiveness to your design. Experimenting with even more complex stitchery adds further dimension to your work. Working the embroidery in a color close in intensity to the background color makes the stitches look "tidier."

Rounded Patches

While straight lines can give an architectural flavor to your design, rounded patches are likely to give the work a much more organic feel. Crochet, in particular, lends itself to working with curves. When creating any design in a totally freeform manner, you do not need to calculate and plan precisely where the joins will be. It is amazing how easy it is to fit a variety of strangely shaped pieces together—just like a puzzle. So grab your hooks or needles, create a few random patches yourself, and give it a try.

Starfish

These star-shaped motifs are quick and easy to crochet. They can be made completely separate from each other and then stitched together later, or they can be joined, point by point, as they are worked. (See page 111 for step-by-step instructions on crocheting starfish.) Make as many as you want in one or more colors, and scatter them in a seemingly random manner on top of your creations. For inspiration, look at how Prudence has used them for *Naturalis*, *Étoile de Mer* or *Flor do Mar* (see the *Starfish Sweaters*, pages 58 through 65).

Leaves

Simple knitted shapes, such as these garter stitch leaves, are another great way to add interest to a plain design. Take a look at how we have added leaflike shapes for embellishment on *Scintilla*, *Izleses* and *Nyskabende* (see the *Basic Tees*, pages 66 through 73). Use the photos of our projects as your starting point, but don't feel bound to stick too closely to what we have done. The more you vary the size, shape and number of your motifs, the more you will be putting your own original stamp on the basic design.

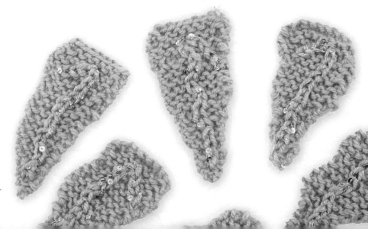

Flowers

Another easy organic motif can be created just by crocheting too many stitches into the one place. If these stitches (in this case, double crochet stitches) are worked in a circle, the resulting piece will soon begin to resemble a flower. Add a second round, again using too many stitches, and watch your blossom burst into life. We added flowers like this to our simple purse design, to create *Fiore di Bambu*, *Bambusblume* and *Bamboe Bloem* (see the *Drawstring Purses*, pages 46 through 51).

Other floral shapes can be created by incorporating petal-shaped sections. These pretty flowers, used on some of our felted hats, are easily made with crochet—this time using just chain and single crochet stitches. (See the techniques section, beginning on page 100, for step-by-step instructions on crochet stitches.)

Both of these crochet floral motifs are simple enough even for beginners. If you are a knitter who has never given crochet a try, why not take this opportunity to see how using a hook can add variety to your knitted creations?

Domes

A dome motif is a good way to literally add another dimension to your freeforming, even when you are working with relatively smooth yarns. Make them separately and scatter them about, or join them to each other or to other crochet pieces to create all manner of interesting textures. Also consider using them upside down, as small cupped shapes.

Creating a crochet dome is really very simple. It's just a matter of working fewer stitches before joining than would be needed to create a circle that will lie flat. When too few stitches are worked around a circle, the piece is forced to pop up in the center (see page 108 for step-by-step instructions on how to crochet domes).

Ruffles

A ruffle can make a pleasing embellishment to a collar, cuff or hemline, and can also be incorporated into the middle of a solid piece. It's an easy embellishment that adds just the right amount of feminine detail.

Ruffles are quite simple to create by quickly increasing the number of stitches from one row to the next. Just as too many crochet stitches worked into a circle make the piece start to flute and ripple, too many stitches worked in a straight line create a ruffled effect. The more stitches worked into any position, or the more rows of increases worked, the more frilly the piece becomes. Ruffles can just as easily be made with knitting—it is simply a matter of increasing one or more stitches into every stitch over a number of rows (see page 114 for step-by-step instructions on how to create ruffles).

Corkscrews

A corkscrew is simply a freestanding ruffle. Instead of increasing from an existing piece, the first row of stitches is rapidly increased from the number of stitches in the beginning chain. The result is that the piece eventually twists around on itself in a corkscrew. These fun motifs make wonderful additions to your freeform repertoire. Take a look at how we have used them on the scarves (see pages 26 through 33) and hats (see pages 34 through 39).

Borders

Edging stitches in either knitting or crochet can be worked as functional borders around the necks, armholes or hems of many garments to neaten an edge, but why not create decorative borders that add even more freeform flair?

Fancy fringing, random zigzags or the addition of a final round of crab stitch crochet will help make your garments stand out from the crowd.

Fringe

You often see lengths of yarn looped through edge stitches to finish off a scarf, but for a more unusual finish you can experiment with some of our other fringing ideas. Prudence often jazzes up the ends of her pieces with knitted I-cord or crochet corkscrews. And when she thinks fringe, she doesn't just think scarves—take a look at how she adds knit or crochet strips to our bamboo A-line skirts (see pages 74 through 79) and purses (see pages 46 through 51) for extra panache.

Zigzags

We think the jagged freeform edging on our *Scintilla* design (see page 68) really makes a statement. Simple to knit, it's worked in garter stitch with random increases and decreases along just one side. It was made as a separate strip and then stitched to the hem of the garment. The use of SWTC's sparkling Yang yarn turned an otherwise basic pattern into a masterpiece for evening wear. Take this zigzag idea and add it anywhere else you wish—around the neck or on the sleeves, or why not sew on a couple of short strips for faux pocket flaps?

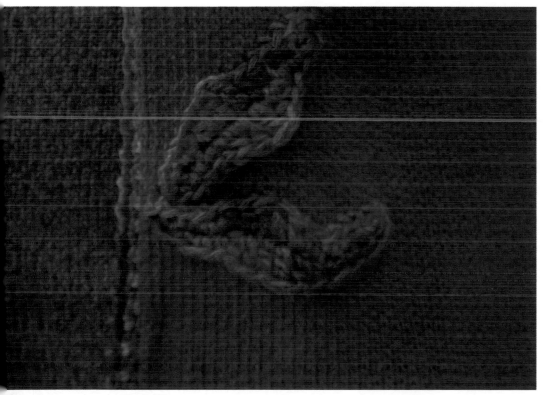

Crab Stitch

Although this is a traditional crochet stitch, many people find it one of the most difficult stitches to master (and remember) because it is worked in the opposite direction to other crochet stitches. Check out our step-by-step directions for right-handed and left-handed crab stitch (see pages 115 and 116). You might find our unusual way of scooping the yarn for the first yarn over helpful, as it sets your hook in the right direction to complete the stitch without inadvertently creating a reverse slip stitch. Although we used crab stitch on just a few of our garments, feel free to add it to any of the edges on your projects, especially if you feel they need to be firmed up a little. Just remember that to get the full effect of the rolled edge, you should always work crab stitch with the right side facing.

The Patterns

Grab your needles and hooks, and join us on a freeform adventure. With these patterns, you'll explore simple stitches and motifs that become eye-catching embellishments. You'll also learn to use color to add drama and interest to your freeform pieces.

A great starting place is the *Magico* design (see page 28), which begins with a simple knit or crochet scarf. You'll learn how to create a fabulous corkscrew fringe combined with reversible oval discs. The result is a wonderful and playful scarf. We are confident this fringe will show up on your future artwork as trims, edgings and embellishment in the years to come.

If you are new to either crochet or knitting, the crochet and knitting *Basics* sections will help you double-check your technique (see pages 100 through 133). If you just need a little extra help, refer to the general instructions in the *Elements of Freeform* section (see pages 14 through 23). There is no shame in needing a refresher course—even fiber arts veterans need a reminder every now and again. Prudence has to show Jonelle the crochet crab stitch again every time she wants to do it!

One of the questions we hear a lot is: "What if my stitches look different than yours?" Pay attention to this answer and remember our first rule: There are no rules. If you like how it looks, regardless of right or wrong, keep going! Jonelle volunteered a great example. For two years, she did her single crochets "wrong." Self-taught and left-handed, she had adapted a sort of hybrid stitch that more closely resembled a half double crochet. Rip it out? Absolutely not! Her funky little stitch made a wonderful freeform element in her pieces and helped to make them all unique.

In the following pages, we present you with ten different projects, each in three different levels. They range from simple accessories, such as our scarves, to wild freeform works of art like *Libertad Artistica* (see page 94), the magnificent freeform cape created by Prudence. If you are new to freeform, start with the *Level 1* projects. The basic knit or crochet garment will be quickly transformed into a freeform masterpiece with our simple instructions. Soon you'll see how easy it is to add freeform knit and crochet elements to any garment using your own artistic flair as your guide.

As you embrace the next step, the *Level 2* projects will have you working with even more stitches, motifs and colors. Again, our instructions can certainly be your guide, but your own creativity will dictate the finished product.

The *Level 3* projects are all you! The directions read more like an overview of the project. We encourage you to embrace your own artistry to make your project magical. All of the wonderful new things you have learned will come into play as you take our basic idea and make it your own. There will always be new and exciting things to discover along the way.

Once you have created a few of the garments in *Freeform Style* and have mastered the techniques we've shared, we hope you will continue to explore their potential in even more freeform creations. Any pattern can be jazzed up with a few spectacular embellishments from your new arsenal of ideas.

Whether you're making a purse, skirt or scarf, these simple techniques are the foundation of freeform art. It is a concept based on freeing yourself from patterns and rules and letting your own personality shine through by using lots of color and creativity in your art. It sounds like magic, but with our simple tricks, you can do it with ease!

The greatest compliment we can receive is to see you succeed in making our ideas come to life with your own flair and unique style. As we've said before, make *Freeform Style* your style. You have our permission!

Fringed Scarves

Make a simple scarf magical with fabulous free-form fringe. Start with our basic scarf patterns in either knit or crochet, and then add any free-form elements you like. For the *Level 1* freeform scarf, simply attach reversible oval discs and corkscrews to create a wild fringe. In the *Level 2* version, you'll learn to add small and large oval circles and use different colors of yarn to create a striking fringe. The *Level 3* scarf uses all of these techniques in numerous colors to create a winter masterpiece.

Project Basics

FINISHED MEASUREMENTS
8" × 50" (20cm × 127cm)

YARN

Level 1:
5 skeins SWTC Inspiration (Soysilk®/alpaca blend, 125 yds [115m] per 50g skein)

Level 2:
As Level 1, plus 1 additional skein of SWTC Inspiration in a contrast color

Level 3:
4 skeins of SWTC Inspiration in main color, plus 1 skein in each of 6 additional contrast colors

NEEDLES AND HOOKS

All levels:
US size 7 (4.5mm) needles
size F (3.75mm) crochet hook

Level 3 only:
1 set of 2 US size 5 (3.75mm) DPNs

NOTIONS
yarn needle

GAUGE
Knit: 20 sts – 4" (10cm) in patt
Crochet: 12 sts = 4" (10cm) in patt

Magico

In Portugal, *magico* means absolutely magical. With an array of reversible discs and corkscrew fringe, your scarf will be magical, too. This basic scarf is a great introduction to freeform. Add as little or as much freeform embellishment as you want.

Level
1

First, choose your basic scarf pattern from either the knit or crochet version below.

KNIT SCARF

With US 7 (4.5mm) needles, CO 41 sts.

Knit 1 row.

Knit 4 rows in seed st (k1, p1) across row to last st, k1.

NEXT ROW: K1, *yo, k2, sl yo over those 2 sts; rep from * across.

NEXT ROW: Purl.

Rep last 2 rows until scarf measures 49" (124cm) long.

Knit 4 rows in seed st as before. BO. Weave in ends.

CROCHET SCARF

With crochet hook, ch 27.

ROW 1: Sc in 4th ch from hook (counts as 1st sc and dc),*dc in next ch, sc in next ch; rep from * to last ch, dc—25 sts. Ch 3, turn.

ROW 2: Work sc over each dc, dc over each sc across.

Rep Row 2 until piece measures 50" (127cm) long. Fasten off. Weave in ends.

FREEFORM EMBELLISHMENTS

REVERSIBLE OVAL DISCS (MAKE 25–30)

With crochet hook, ch 3 and join with sl st to form a ring. Ch 1, and into the ring work 2 sc, 2 hdc, 4 dc, 2 hdc, 2 sc. Join with sl st, fasten off.

Make another motif in the same manner, but this time do not cut the working yarn after the closing sl st.

Hold the 2 motifs together with RS facing outward, and join them by working a row of crochet around the outside as foll: slip the crochet hook out of the loop, insert the hook into the back loop of the last dc worked on the other disc, pick up the loop again and pull it through. *Ch 1, sc in back loop of each of the next sts on each disc. Rep from * around to join the discs. Do not cut off yarn, but make a length of chain double the desired fringe length (between 60 to 100 ch). Skip the 1st ch

and work 3 sc into the next ch. (See page 120 for step-by-step instructions on joining for crocheting reversible oval discs).

Cont working 3 sc into each of the next 10 to 20 ch to create a corkscrew on the end of the fringe. (See page 110 for step-by-step instructions on crocheting corkscrews.) When corkscrew is desired size, skip the next ch and sl st into the following ch. Fasten off and weave in ends.

FINISHING

To attach the fringe, fold each one off center so the disc and the corkscrew fall at different lengths, insert crochet hook into a st at the end of the scarf, pull through the ch at the fold point to create a loop, drop the ends of the fringe through the loop, and pull down to secure. Attach remaining fringe in same manner, spaced evenly on both ends of the scarf (see page 122 for step-by-step instructions for attaching fringe).

Tip

Once you have made several lengths of fringe, you needn't be so particular about keeping count of your stitches. The more random your pieces, the more freeform your creation will be. You might like to vary the size or shape of some of the discs. (You just need to keep the "pairs" reasonably close in size for ease in joining.) You can also change the size of a few of the corkscrews by substituting half-double crochet or double crochet for the single crochet stitches or try working fewer (or more) stitches into each chain when making some of the corkscrews to create pieces that are either less or more twisty.

Verzauberung

The German word for enchantment is *Verzauberung*, and this scarf will certainly cast its spell on you! This scarf builds on the embellishments used for *Level 1* to take it to a new level.

Level

2

Knit or crochet the base scarf as for Level 1 (see page 29 for the pattern). If desired, add 1 skein of SWTC Inspiration yarn in a second color. Denote one color as "A" and the other as "B."

FREEFORM EMBELLISHMENTS

SMALL OPEN CIRCLES (MAKE 6–10)

Wrap yarn A around your index finger a number of times to create a padded center. Slip the yarn off your finger, ch 1, and then work as many dc around the ring as it takes to fill it solidly enough so that it lies flat. Join with sl st. With yarn B, work a rnd of sl sts into the front loop of each of the dc, sl st to join, and fasten off. Turn the piece over and work another rnd of sl sts into the back loops so B shows up on both sides of the scarf (see page 107 for step-by-step instructions on crocheting an open circle).

LARGE OPEN CIRCLES (MAKE 5–7)

Work as for Small Open Circles, adding an additional 1–2 rnds of dc before working contrast rounds, increasing as needed to keep motif flat.

DELUXE REVERSIBLE OVAL DISCS (MAKE 25–30)

With yarn B, make 2 Reversible Oval Discs as for Level 1. Join as follows:

With yarn A, slip the crochet hook out of the loop, insert the hook into the back loop of the last dc worked on the other disc, pick up the loop again and pull it through. Ch 5, *dc into the back loops of the next st on both discs to join them together, ch 2. Rep from * around, sl st to join. Ch 1, then work 3 or 4 hdc into each of the ch-2 spaces to create a solid rim around the motif. Sl st to join. Work corkscrew fringe as for Level 1. Fasten off.

With yarn B, work rnds of sl sts into the front loops of the dc sts around the motif. Then turn the motif over and do the same into the back loops that will now be facing you on the other side. Weave in ends (see page 108 for step-by-step instructions on crocheting slip stitch).

FINISHING

Arrange circles as desired at ends of scarf, sew in place. Join fringe as for Level 1.

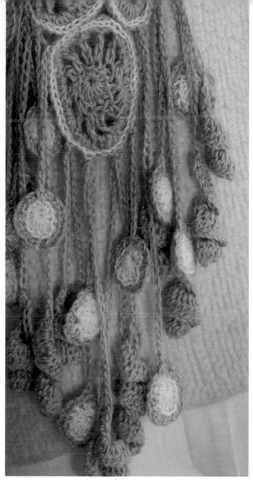

If you feel you need to add a few filler stitches anywhere to help the design come together, or to close a gap, trust your own judgment and do it!

Magia

In Poland, *magia* is the word for magical. *Level 3* explodes with color as the fringe used in the previous levels is taken to the extreme. Let loose and feel the power!

Level
3

Knit or crochet the base scarf as for Level 1 (see page 29 for the pattern). For this version, you need only 4 skeins of Inspiration yarn in the main color and 1 skein each of 6 additional colors.

FREEFORM EMBELLISHMENTS

Using techniques from Levels 1 and 2 and additional colors of yarn, create as many Small and Large Open Circles and Reversible Oval Discs as desired.

Change color within any of the motifs as the fancy takes you. With your fully freeform version, you can let yourself go as much as you wish, even including other motifs not specified here, should you wish to do so.

TUBULAR (I-CORD) KNIT FRINGE
(MAKE 40–50)

Using DPNs and desired color, CO 4 sts and knit 1 row. Do not turn the work, but instead slip the sts to the other end of the needle. The yarn you are working with will be at the wrong end of the needle, so pull it tightly across the back of the work to put it into the correct position for knitting, and knit the next row. Then again push the sts to the other end, pull the yarn across the back as before and knit another row. Continue in this fashion until the tubular fringe measures 10" to 20" (25cm to 51cm) or desired length. Bind off by cutting yarn and drawing tail tight through all sts (see page 129 for step-by-step instructions on knitting I-cord).

FINISHING

You may attach the fringe motifs any way you like. You could choose to join them all together as each motif is completed, or you might wish to add other random sts to the edge of some motifs once they are joined. Strike a happy medium (between making every single motif separately, or joining pieces constantly until the scarf is complete) by building up your design using small patches. Join a few motifs together, but as soon as you feel that you do not quite know what to do next, stop working on that piece and start another. Eventually you can stitch all of the sections together, or join them using random crochet chains. Weave in ends.

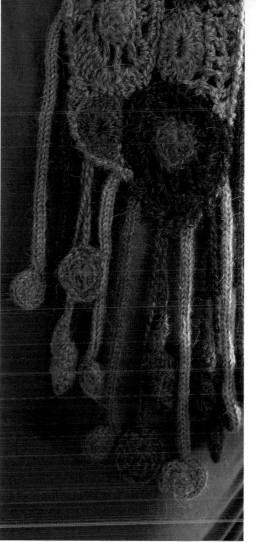

Tip

Where the pieces do not fit perfectly you can leave small spaces, fill in larger gaps with a variety of different stitches, or add small sections of crochet mesh. Having some "holes" between the heavier motifs will help to give a fully freeformed scarf good drape. If you are concerned that the shaping of your scarf will not stay on track, create a long narrow template from paper or waste fabric so that you can periodically place your work on top of this pattern to check on your progress. Or create your own unique template in whatever shape and size you desire for an even more adventurous scarf.

Panel Hats

Each of these three hats combines roughly triangular panels of felted fabric with freeform embellishments. At first glance, these hats seem a bit complicated, but they're actually far easier than they look. If you've never tried felting (or done it by accident), your home washing machine will do the work. All you have to do is send the knitted fabric through a hot cycle. The embellishments that connect the panels and decorate the hats are also surprisingly easy. The *Level 1* hat uses deceptively simple chain stitching to form a lacy design. In the *Level 2* hat, you'll learn to add whimsical corkscrews to the top and delicate flowers to the sides. In *Level 3*, the freeform embellishments take the shape of playful and feminine ruffles. Once you get the picture of how these hats are created, you can seam the panels together with any sort of freeform crochet you like.

Project Basics

SIZES
Women's medium

FINISHED MEASUREMENTS
22" (56cm) head circumference
(after felting)

YARN
All Levels:
3 skeins SWTC Karaoke (Soysilk®/wool blend, 109 yds [100m] per 50g skein) (A)

1 skein SWTC Tofutsies (superwash wool/Soysilk®/cotton/chitin blend, 464 yds [425m] per 100g skein) (B)

(Our Level 1 hat was embellished with SWTC Bamboo, and Levels 2 and 3 were embellished with SWTC Tofutsies. Choose whichever yarn you prefer for any level based on the color you desire.)

NEEDLES AND HOOKS
All levels:
US size 7 (4.5mm) needles
size B (2.25mm) crochet hook

NOTIONS
yarn needle

GAUGE
20 sts = 4" (10cm) in pattern using yarn A (before felting)

Hat and Soul

The *Level 1* hat looks like the most difficult of them all, but that intricate lace is just random chain stitching. Deceptively simple yet excitingly beautiful is our goal—and we've certainly achieved it with *Hat and Soul*.

Level
1

FELTED HAT

Using yarn A, CO 72 sts. Work in St st for 30" (76cm). Bind off.

FELTING

Felt until piece measures approximately 12" × 25" (30cm × 64cm). Lay flat and allow to dry completely.

ASSEMBLY

Enlarge the template at right and trace the appropriate outline onto a piece of heavy paper or cardboard. Use the pattern to cut 5 identical panels from the felted rectangle.

BASE ROUND

Using a crochet hook and yarn B, work a rnd of [sc, ch 1] evenly spaced around the edge of each piece. (See page 117 for step-by-step instructions on crocheting through felted fabric.) Fasten off.

Holding 2 hat panels with WS tog, use yarn B to work a row of sc sts into the edging, working through sts on both panels at once to seam them tog. Both the sc and the ch-1 sp in the previous rnd count as sts when joining. Adjust as needed to keep fabric smooth and free from puckers. Cont as est with rem panels. Weave in ends.

FREEFORM EMBELLISHMENTS

LACE

Rejoin yarn B at lower corner of first panel. Ch desired number of sts and join close to beg of ch to make a loop on the surface of the panel. Cont working over the surface of the piece, randomly making ch sts and connecting them either to edging sts or previous ch to make a lacy freeform mesh all over the surface of the felted panel. Keep an eye on how things are progressing as you add each new section of crochet to ensure the desired result. Rep on rem panels. Weave in ends.

Hat Patterns

Level 3 Hat Pattern

Level 1 Hat Pattern

Level 2 Hat Pattern

Enlarge template by 143% to bring to full size. Use this template for each of the panels.

Sombrero y Alma

Karaoke yarn again takes the stage in *Sombrero y Alma*, which is Spanish for hat and soul. You've never seen a sombrero like this! Prudence added whimsical corkscrews to the top and delicate flowers to the sides, and instead of hiding the seams, they're integrated into the hat, making the mere act of sewing the pieces together a key design element. Another rule broken!

Level
2

Create the felted hat as for Level 1 (see page 37 for the pattern). All materials and size information are the same as for the Level 1 hat, but use the Level 2 template.

FREEFORM EMBELLISHMENTS

RANDOM CROCHET FLOWERS AND SMALL BOBBLES (MAKE AS MANY AS DESIRED)

Using a crochet hook and yarn B, ch 3 and join with a sl st to form a ring.

RND 1: *Ch 5, sl st into the ring. Rep from * 4 more times (5 petal loops made).

RND 2: Work sufficient hdc sts into the first petal loop to fill it well, then make 1 sl st back into the ring. Rep to fill each of the other petal loops. Fasten off.

If desired, add a small bobble to the center of each flower, plus add other random bobbles anywhere you feel they are needed to help balance your freeform design. (See page 109 for step-by-step instructions on how to crochet bobbles.)

CORKSCREWS (MAKE AS MANY AS DESIRED)

Using a crochet hook and yarn B, crochet a ch approx the length desired for the corkscrew. Skip the first ch, and work 3 sc into each rem ch. Fasten off.

FINISHING

Sew flowers as desired over surface of hat. Stitch corkscrews in position at crown of hat. Weave in ends.

Cappello e l'Anima

In Italian, hat and soul translates to *Cappello e l'Anima*. This hat explores ruffles, a feminine detail long relegated to the bottoms of children's skirts. No more! Prudence gives ruffles a new place at the top of our heads and hearts with a creative ruffly finish on this wonderful hat. Show your personality and shape your felt any way that suits you. Try a narrow top or maybe a slightly more domed shape. Jonelle likes hats that sit lower on her face, and Prudence loves hats that draw your eye to the embellishments on the top. It's all about your personality with a hat! After you've dreamed up your foundation, it can become the canvas for your art. Use lacy freeform stitches to create an interesting web or to add more flowers and ruffles. If you like an embellishment from an earlier project, add it to your hat and see where it leads you.

Create the felted hat as for Level 1 (see page 37 for the pattern). All materials and size information are the same as for the Level 1 hat, but use the Level 3 template.

FREEFORM EMBELLISHMENTS

RUFFLES

Using a crochet hook and yarn B, work multiple crochet sts into each of the sts used to join the panels. The number and height of the sts used are entirely up to you—try dc, trc...anything! You may like to keep the sts consistent throughout, or change them randomly as you work for a more unusual and organic ruffle. The more sts placed in the same area, the frillier that section of the ruffle will be. The taller the sts used, the farther the ruffle will stand out from the surface of the hat. You might even like to add a second row of sts to the ruffle, increasing sts in this second row as desired. This second row of sts could be the same height as the first row, or a different height. Weave in ends (see page 114 for step-by-step instructions on crocheting a ruffle).

Level 3

Cabled Gloves

The classic styling of these gloves makes a great foundation for freeform embellishment. The basic pattern for the main part of these gloves is the same for all three levels, and so are the dome stitches on the cuffs. Once you master the domes, take the next step and give the *Level 2* or *3* gloves a try and create longer, more dramatic cuffs. This is a great place to gain confidence in your freeforming so you'll be ready to take on some of the other amazing projects that lie ahead. Trust your artistry…you can do great things.

Project Basics

FINISHED MEASUREMENTS

7" (18cm) hand circumference at widest part of hand

YARN

All levels:

2 skeins SWTC Yin (wool/silk/bamboo blend, 167 yds [150m] per 50g skein) (A)

1 skein SWTC Yin (wool/silk/bamboo blend, 167 yds [150m] per 50g skein), in 2 to 4 additional colors, as desired, for the freeform embellishment

NEEDLES AND HOOKS

All levels:

1 set of 5 US size 5 (3.75mm) DPNs
size F (3.75mm) crochet hook

NOTIONS

2 stitch markers
4 small stitch holders
yarn needle

GAUGE

24 sts and 28 rows = 4" (10cm) in St st

BASIC GLOVE PATTERN (ALL LEVELS)

Follow this pattern to make the main part of the glove for each level.

LACE PATTERN STITCH

RNDS 1–2: * P2, k3; rep from * to last 2 sts, p2.

RND 3: * P2, slip 3rd knit st on left needle over other 2 knit sts, then knit those 2 sts; rep from * to last 2 sts, p2.

RND 4: * P2, k1, yo, k1; rep from * to last 2 sts, p2.

Rep rnds 1–4 for patt.

Notes: The glove pattern begins at the top of the wrist, and the cuff is added with freeform embellishment after the knitting is complete.

LOWER HAND (BOTH GLOVES)

With yarn A, CO 43 sts. Join, being careful not to twist sts. Knit 1 rnd.

Work lace patt over 22 sts for back of hand, work rem 21 sts in St st for palm. Work even as est for 12 rnds.

THUMB GUSSET (RIGHT HAND)

RND 1: Work Row 1 of lace patt to last 2 purl sts, pm, p1, M1, p1, pm, work St st to end of rnd.

Cont in lace patt and St st as est, inc as foll between markers for thumb gusset:

RND 2: M1, k3, M1.

RND 3: M1, p1, pass 3rd knit st over 2 sts, then knit those 2 sts, p1, M1.

RND 4: P2, k1, yo, k1, p2.

RND 5: M1, p2, k3, p2, M1.

RND 6: P3, k3, p2, k1.

RND 7: M1, p3, pass 3rd knit st over 2 sts, then knit those 2 sts, p2, k1, M1.

RND 8: P4, k1, yo, k1, p2, k2.

RND 9: M1, p1, k1, p2, k3, p2, k2, M1.

RND 10: P2, k1, p2, k3, p2, k3.

RND 11: M1, p1, k2, p2, pass 3rd st. over 2 sts and knit those 2 sts, p2, k3, M1.

RND 12: P2, k2, p2, k1, yo, k1, p2, k4—15 gusset sts between markers.

Cont in patt without inc until gusset measures 2¾" (7cm).

Work across back of hand sts, place thumb gusset sts on 2 holders, CO 2 sts to bridge gap, knit across palm sts—43 hand sts.

Cont in patt, purling over the 2 cast-on sts, working until hand measures 3½" (9cm) from start of thumb gusset.

LITTLE FINGER
Keeping in patt as est, work across 6 sts, place next 33 sts on 2 holders, CO 2 sts to bridge gap, k4—12 sts.

NEXT RND: Work in rnd on these sts in est patt (p1, k1) over cast-on sts until little finger measures 2¼" (6cm).

NEXT RND: K2tog across—6 sts.

Cut yarn and run tail through rem sts to close. Weave in tail.

UPPER HAND
Reattach yarn at base of little finger on back of hand, work in patt across back of hand, knit palm sts, pick up 2 sts at base of little finger—35 sts.

Knit 1 more rnd in patt (k1, p1 over picked-up sts).

RING FINGER
Work over next 5 sts, place next 23 sts on 2 holders, CO 2 sts to bridge gap, work across rem 7 sts—14 sts.

Work in patt (p1, k1 over cast-on sts) until finger measures 2½" (6cm). Complete as for little finger.

MIDDLE FINGER
Reattach yarn at base of ring finger on back of hand. Work across 5 sts, place 13 sts on holder, CO 2 sts to bridge gap, work across rem 5 sts, pick up 2 sts at base of ring finger—14 sts.

Keep in patt (p1, k1 over cast-on sts and k1, p1 over picked-up sts), work until finger measures 3" (8cm). Complete as for little finger.

INDEX FINGER
Reattach yarn at base of middle finger on back of

hand. Work across 13 sts, pick up 2 sts at base of middle finger—15 sts.

Keeping in patt (k1, p1 over picked-up sts) work until finger measures 2¾" (7cm). Complete as for little finger, working k1 at end of last rnd.

THUMB
Reattach yarn at base of thumb on back of hand. Work 15 sts, pick up 2 sts at base of thumb opening—17 sts.

Maintain lace patt up thumb (p2, k3, p2 section) while keeping rem sts in St st. Work until thumb measures 2" (5cm).

NEXT RND: K2tog around, end k1—9 sts.

NEXT RND: K2tog around, end k1—5 sts.

Cut yarn and thread through rem sts to close. Weave in ends.

THUMB GUSSET (LEFT GLOVE)
Work lower hand as for right glove.

RND 1: Pm, p1, M1, p1, pm. Cont in lace patt for back of hand and St st for palm.

Inc between markers as foll for thumb gusset:

RND 2: M1, k3, M1.

RND 3: M1, p1, slip 3rd st over 2 sts, then knit those 2 sts, p1, M1.

RND 4: P2, k1, yo, k1, p2.

RND 5: M1, p2, k3, p2, M1.

RND 6: K1, p2, k3, p3.

RND 7: M1, k1, p2, slip 3rd st over 2 sts then knit those 2 sts, p4, M1.

RND 8: K2, p2, k1, yo, k1, p4.

RND 9: M1, k3, p2, k3, p2, k1, p1, M1.

RND 10: K3, p2, k3, p2, k1, p2.

RND 11: M1, k3, p2, slip 3rd st over 2 sts, then knit those 2 sts, p2, k2, p1, M1.

RND 12: K4, p2, k1, yo, k1, p2, k2, p2—15 gusset sts between markers.

Cont in patt without inc until gusset measures 2¾" (7cm).

Work across palm sts, place thumb gusset sts on 2 holders, CO 2 sts to bridge gap, work across back sts—43 hand sts.

Keeping in patt and purling over the 2 cast-on sts, work until hand measures 3½" (9cm) from start of thumb gusset.

LITTLE FINGER
Work across 4 sts, place next 33 sts on 2 holders, CO 2 sts to bridge gap, work across rem 6 sts—12 sts.

Keeping in patt (k1, p1 over cast-on sts), complete as for right glove little finger.

UPPER HAND
Reattach yarn at base of little finger on palm side. Work 1 rnd in patt, pick up 2 sts at base of little finger. Complete 1 more rnd (p1, k1 over picked-up sts).

RING FINGER
Work over next 7 sts, place 23 sts on holders. CO 2 sts to bridge gap, work across rem 5 sts—14 sts.

Keeping in patt (k1, p1 over cast-on sts), complete as for right glove.

MIDDLE FINGER
Reattach yarn at base of ring finger on palm side. Work across 5 sts, place 13 sts on holder, CO 2 sts to bridge gap, work across rem 5 sts, pick up 2 sts at base of ring finger—14 sts.

Keeping in patt (k1, p1 over cast-on sts and p1, k1 over picked-up sts), complete as for right glove.

INDEX FINGER
Reattach yarn at base of middle finger on palm side. Work across 13 sts, pick up 2 sts at base of middle finger—15 sts.

Keeping in patt (p1, k1 over picked-up sts), complete as for right glove.

THUMB
Reattach yarn at base of thumb on palm side. Work across 15 sts, pick up 2 sts at base of thumb opening—17 sts.

Complete as for right glove.

FINISHING
Weave in ends.

Kreativitat

When in Germany, you'll hear *kreativitat* when they're talking creative. We've taken Yin, the wonderful SWTC bamboo, wool and silk blend yarn and knit it into a glove inspired by a vintage riding glove. With added bobbles and color, Prudence transforms a basic glove into something...*kreativitat*.

Level
1

Follow the pattern beginning on page 41 to knit the gloves. Then add a freeform cuff as follows.

FREEFORM CUFF

CROCHET DOMES (MAKE 25–30)

With crochet hook and desired color, ch 3 and join with a sl st to form a ring. Ch 3 again and work 6 dc into the ring. Join with a sl st to the top of ch 3 to close, fasten off. Because not enough sts have been worked for the piece to lay flat, it will pop up once joined, creating a small dome-like shape (see page 108 for step-by-step instructions on crocheting domes).

ASSEMBLY

Arrange domes in approx 2 rnds to create a cuff on each glove. Sew the domes tog from the WS, or join them as they are made by holding the RS of 2 domes tog and attaching them from the WS using a couple of sc sts. Weave in ends.

Inspiration

We use the word inspiration a lot. For an artist, the inspiration can be anything! The *Level 2* gloves use the basic glove pattern, but incorporate more colors and more domes to lengthen the cuffs. Our directions here are simple—make the gloves your own. Whether you line up your domes by color, within symmetrical lines or create a unique shape, the result will be a pair of warm and wonderful gloves.

Level **2**

Follow the pattern beginning on page 41 to knit the gloves. Then create a freeform cuff as follows.

FREEFORM CUFF

CROCHET DOMES (MAKE 40–50)

Make crochet domes just as for the Level 1 gloves, but use even more colors (see page 108 for step-by-step instructions on creating domes).

ASSEMBLY

Arrange domes in approx 4 rnds to create a cuff on each glove. Sew the domes tog from the WS, or join them as they are made by holding the RS of 2 domes tog and attaching them from the WS using a couple of sc sts. Weave in ends.

Using crochet hook and yarn A, sc around the edge of cuff to help bring colors tog and finish the project. Weave in ends.

Belleza

Belleza is the Spanish word for beauty. Our vintage gloves have now become longer and more dramatic with rows of brightly colored domes held together with random crochet work. Can they be even longer? You bet. Make them elbow length. Make gauntlets. Make anything you want! We'll tell you throughout the book that freeform has no rules, no pattern and no mistakes. Whether you prefer simple and elegant or wild and dramatic, the glove is merely the foundation for the rest of your vision. Use one color or many; use ten domes or one hundred. Challenge yourself to be truly unique here, and create a glove that you will treasure.

Follow the pattern beginning on page 41 to knit the gloves. Then create a freeform cuff as follows.

FREEFORM CUFF

CROCHET DOMES (MAKE 60 OR MORE)

Make crochet domes as for the Level 1 and Level 2 gloves, using as many colors as you desire (see page 108 for step-by-step instructions on creating domes).

Surround each dome with a variety of random crochet sts to add drama.

ASSEMBLY

Work as for Levels 1 and 2, making the cuffs as long as you want.

Using crochet hook and yarn A, sc around the edge of cuff to help bring colors tog and finish the project. Weave in ends.

Level

3

Drawstring Purses

We wanted to create an easy purse project that coould be a foundation for either an everyday bag or a fantastic evening accessory. We wanted it to be fabulous for girls young and old. We wanted it to be simple, yet fun. With SWTC Bamboo yarn and over forty colors to choose from, we achieved our goal. This project, in all thrcc levels, starts with a simple purse that is knit in one piece. When folded and sewn, it is self lining, wich adds reinforcement for all that "stuff" we tote around. Jonelle tried hers out, and once the lipstick and essentials were in she proudly added her small knitting project and declared it a perfect purse.

Project Basics

FINISHED MEASUREMENTS

7" × 7½" (18cm × 19cm)

YARN

All levels:

1 skein SWTC Bamboo (bamboo, 250 yds [228m] per 100g skein)

Levels 2 and 3:

Additional small quantities of SWTC Bamboo in one or more contrasting colors as desired.

NEEDLES AND HOOKS

All levels:

US size 6 (4mm) needles

1 set of 2 US size 5 (3.75mm) DPNs for the drawstring handles

size F (3.75mm) crochet hook

NOTIONS

yarn needle

GAUGE

20 sts and 32 rows= 4" (10cm) in St st

Fiore di Bambu

Bamboo is beautiful in any language, but it sounds particularly elegant in Italian. Our first purse project is *Fiore di Bambu*, or Bamboo Flower, named for the elegant crochet flowers that adorn it. Using variegated bamboo yarn, Prudence created a simple rectangle as the canvas for more freeform fun, turning it into a lined purse with an added I-cord drawstring. This is another great project for beginners. Use our simple ideas and then cut loose with your own style!

Level **1**

PURSE

CO 35 sts. Work in St st until piece measures 30" (76cm). BO.

ASSEMBLY

Fold CO and BO to center, sew tog. Fold piece in half again so that seam is at inside bottom of purse. Measure ½" (1cm) down from top edge of purse on each side. Sew side seams (both inside and outside) up to this mark. To form casing for drawstring, sew across top edges at markers on both sides. Weave in ends. Turn right side out.

I-CORD DRAWSTRING (MAKE 2)

Using DPNs and desired color, CO 4 sts and knit 1 row. Do not turn the work, but instead slip the sts to the other end of the needle. The yarn you are working with will be at the wrong end of the needle, so pull it tightly across the back of the work to put it into the correct position for knitting, and knit the next row. Then again push the sts to the other end, pull the yarn across the back as before and knit another row. Cont in this fashion until drawstring measures 60" (152cm). Bind off by cutting yarn and drawing tail tight through all sts (see page 129 for step-by-step instructions for knitting I-cord).

Insert first cord through casing with ends hanging evenly on left side of purse, insert second cord through the opposite direction with ends hanging evenly on right side of purse. Sew each pair of ends tog to form loops.

FREEFORM EMBELLISHMENTS

FRINGE (MAKE 3 OR MORE)

KNIT METHOD: CO the desired number of sts. Knit 1 row. BO.

CROCHET METHOD: Ch the desired number of sts. Sc in 2nd ch from hook and each ch to end. Fasten off.

Cut yarn, leaving a long enough tail to tie or sew to purse. (See page 122 for step-by-step instructions for creating small bunches of fringe. Working in this manner will simplify the joining).

SINGLE COLOR FLOWER (MAKE 1 OR MORE)

RND 1: Ch 3, and join with sl st to form a small ring. Ch 3, work approx 15 dc into the ring. Sl st to close.

RND 2: Ch 3 and work 5 or 6 dc into each dc in the previous rnd. Sl st to close, fasten off. Be sure to work sufficient sts in the 2nd rnd to cause the piece to ruffle softly so that it forms an attractive, flowerlike motif (see page 112 for step-by-step instructions for creating ruffled-edge flowers).

FINISHING

Once you have made sufficient embellishments (both fringe and flowers), arrange them wherever you desire and then attach either by tying or stitching them neatly into place. Weave in ends.

When sewing the casing, insert a pencil or knitting needle into the fold to create a guide to help you sew a straight seam.

Bambusblume

We loved the name Bamboo Flower and found a beautiful translation in German: *Bambusblume*. For this version of the purse, you'll follow the same basic instructions as for *Level 1*, but add more color and more of each embellishment. Experiment with all of these and try your own ideas on color and placement. Love fringe? Add a lot of it. The little flowers that Prudence designed for this project are addictive. Once you start on them, you'll quickly find a garden of these little beauties in your stash. No worries! Set extras aside. Once you let freeform into your repertoire, you will find there is never a scrap of yarn that can't become something magical down the road.

Level
2

Create the purse as for Level 1 (see page 49 for the pattern). Basic materials and measurements are the same as for the Level 1 purse. Add 1 skein of SWTC Bamboo in a second color, if desired.

FREEFORM EMBELLISHMENTS

FRINGE (MAKE 30 OR MORE)

Make the fringe as for Level 1 (see page 49).

MULTICOLOR FLOWER (MAKE 8 OR MORE)

Work the flowers as for Level 1 (see page 49), changing color for Rnd 2.

FINISHING

Once you have finished making all your embellishments, arrange them on the purse, paying special attention to juxtaposition of color. Attach the flowers and fringe to the purse either by tying or stitching them neatly into place. Weave in ends.

Bamboe Bloem

See the theme? The name *Bamboe Bloem* comes to us from the Netherlands where flowers abound! In *Levels 1* and *2*, you mastered the basic purse, the simple flowers and then frolicked with fun fringe. Now, unleash! Add a ton of fringe, and as many colorful flowers as you want. Lay them out symmetrically or in a completely random way. You can't go wrong! We loved the gentle swish of the fringe when we used the bags. You'll find the fringe again in the A-line skirt patterns (see pages 74 through 79). We just couldn't resist.

Create the purse as for Level 1 (see page 49 for the pattern). Basic materials and measurements are the same as for the Level 1 purse. Add skeins of SWTC Bamboo in multiple colors, if desired.

FREEFORM EMBELLISHMENTS

FRINGE (MAKE 60 OR MORE)

Using a variety of different colors if desired, make fringe as for Level 1 (see page 49)

MULTICOLOR FLOWER (MAKE 17 OR MORE)

Work the flowers as for Level 1 (see page 49), changing color for Rnd 2.

FINISHING

Attach the flowers and fringe to the purse as for the Level 1 and 2 purses, packing in as many as you like.

Level **3**

Tie-Front Vests

Start by knitting this elegant vest in SWTC Bamboo yarn. The sizes are generous and the length can be whatever you want, although you can certainly follow the pattern as given.

BASIC VEST PATTERN (ALL LEVELS)
BACK

CO 152 (166, 180, 194, 208, 222, 236) sts. Work in St st for 2" (5cm), ending with a WS row.

NEXT (DEC) Row (RS): K1, ssk, knit to last 3 sts, k2tog, k1. Rep dec row every 4th row a total of 20 times—112 (126, 140, 154, 168, 182, 196) sts.

Work even until piece measures 12" (30cm) from beg, ending with a WS row. (This is the Level 1 measurement. For Level 2 your piece will need to measure 16" [41cm] and for Level 3 the measurement will be 36" [91cm]).

ARMHOLE SHAPING

BO 10 (10, 12, 15, 17, 18, 20) sts at beg of next 2 rows.

Dec 1 st each side every RS row a total of 6 (7, 8, 9, 10, 11, 12) times—80 (92, 100, 106, 114, 124, 132) sts.

Work even until armhole measures 9 (9½, 10, 10½, 11, 11½, 12)" (23 [24, 25, 27, 28, 29, 30]cm), ending with a WS row.

NECK AND SHOULDER SHAPING

NEXT ROW (RS): Knit across 23 (27, 29, 30, 32, 35, 37) sts, join another ball of yarn and bind off center 34 (38, 42, 46, 50, 54, 58) sts, knit across rem 23 (27, 29, 30, 32, 35, 37) sts. Working both sides separately, dec 1 st at each neck edge once. AT THE SAME TIME, BO 7 (8, 9, 9, 10, 11, 12) sts at shoulder edge at beg of next 4 rows, then BO 8 (10, 10, 11, 11, 12, 12) sts at beg of foll 2 rows.

LEFT FRONT

With yarn A, CO 76 (83, 90, 97, 104, 111, 118) sts. Work in St st for 2" (5cm), ending with a WS row.

NEXT (DEC) Row (RS): K1, ssk, knit to end. Rep dec row every 4th row a total of 20 times—56 (63, 70, 77, 84, 91, 98) sts.

Work even until piece measures 12" (30cm) from beg, ending with a WS row. (This is the Level 1 measurement. For Level 2 your piece will need to measure 16" [41cm] and for Level 3 the measurement will be 36" [91cm]).

ARMHOLE AND NECK SHAPING

BO 10 (10, 12, 15, 17, 18, 20) sts at beg of next row.

Dec 1 st at beg of every RS row a total of 6 (7, 8, 9, 10, 11, 12) times—40 (46, 50, 53, 57, 62, 66) sts.

Cont to work even. When armhole measures 5" (13cm), beg neckline shaping by dec 1 st at neck edge every RS row 18 (20, 22, 24, 26, 28, 30) times—22 (26, 28, 29, 31, 34, 36) sts.

Work even until armhole measures 9 (9½, 10, 10½, 11, 11½, 12)" (23 [24, 25, 27, 28, 29, 30]cm), ending with a WS row.

SHOULDER SHAPING

BO 7 (8, 9, 9, 10, 11, 12) sts at shoulder edge at beg of next 2 RS rows, then BO 8 (10, 10, 11, 11, 12, 12) sts at beg of foll RS row.

RIGHT FRONT

Work as for left front, reversing shaping.

TIES (MAKE 2)

With DPNs, CO 4 sts. Work in I-cord for 30" (76cm). BO. Sew one end to vest fronts at beg of neck dec. Tie an overhand knot at opposite ends.

FINISHING

Sew shoulder and side seams. Weave in ends.

Project Basics

SIZES
Women's XS (S, M, L, XL, 2X, 3X)

FINISHED MEASUREMENTS
Bust: 32 (36, 40, 44, 48, 52, 56)" (81 [91, 102, 112, 122, 132, 142]cm)

Length:

Level 1: 21 (21½, 22, 22½, 23, 23½, 24)" (53 [55, 56, 57, 58, 60, 61]cm)

Level 2: 25 (25½, 26, 26½, 27, 27½, 28)" (64 [65, 66, 67, 69, 70, 71]cm)

Level 3: 45 (45½, 46, 46½, 47, 47½, 48)" (114 [116, 117, 118, 119, 121, 122]cm)

YARN
Level 1: 5 (5, 6, 6, 7, 7, 8) skeins SWTC Bamboo (100% bamboo, 250 yds [228m] per 100g skein) (A)

Level 2: 5 (5, 6, 6, 7, 7, 8) skeins SWTC Bamboo

Level 3: 9 (10, 11, 12, 13, 14, 15) skeins SWTC Bamboo

1 skein SWTC Bamboo in each of 5 additional colors

NEEDLES AND HOOKS
All levels:
US size 6 (4mm) straight needles and 1 set of 2 DPNs

size F (3.75mm) crochet hook

NOTIONS
yarn needle

GAUGE
28 sts and 36 rows = 4" (10cm) in St st

Schematic for vests on page 55

Divatos

In Hungary, *divatos* means "fashionable and trendy." In bamboo, it's just plain gorgeous. Freeform crochet leaves add captivating detail to this simple, basic vest. Make sure to practice the freeform lace technique that graces the bottom of the vest. It's a great technique to master and use in all of your future freeform adventures.

Level
1

Follow the pattern on page 53 to knit the Level 1 vest.

FREEFORM EMBELLISHMENTS

We'll keep our freeform simple in this elegant vest featuring an assortment of leaves in different sizes. In our example, we made 3 small leaves, 6 medium leaves and 9 large leaves. Make as few or as many as you desire!

SMALL LEAF

Ch 15.

ROW 1: Skip the first ch, 1 sc into each of the next 4 ch, 1 hdc into each of the next 2 ch, 1 dc into each of the next 2 ch, 1 hdc into each of the next 2 ch, 1 sc into each of the last 4 ch.

Do not turn the work over. Ch 1, then work Row 2 back along the other side of the foundation ch as foll:

ROW 2: 1 sc into each of the first 4 ch, 1 hdc into each of the next 2 ch, 1 dc into each of the next 2 ch, 1 hdc into each of the next 2 ch, 1 sc into the last 4 ch. Sl st to close, and fasten off leaving a tail for sewing that is at least 3 times the length of the leaf.

MEDIUM LEAF

Ch 20.

ROW 1: Skip the first ch, 1 sc into each of the next 5 ch, 1 hdc into each of the next 2 ch, 1 dc into each of the next 5 ch, 1 hdc into each of the next 2 ch, 1 sc into each of the last 5 ch.

Do not turn the work over. Ch 1, then work Row 2 back along the other side of the foundation ch as foll:

ROW 2: 1 sc into each of the first 5 ch, 1 hdc into each of the next 2 ch, 1 dc into each of the next 5 ch, 1 hdc into each of the next 2 ch, 1 sc into the last 5 ch. Sl st to close, and fasten off leaving a tail for sewing that is at least 3 times the length of the leaf.

LARGE LEAF

Ch 25.

ROW 1: Skip the first ch, 1 sc into each of the next 7 ch, 1 hdc into each of the next 2 ch, 1 dc into each of the next 6 ch, 1 hdc into each of the

next 2 ch, 1 sc into each of the last 7 ch.

Do not turn the work over. Ch 1, then work Row 2 back along the other side of the foundation ch as foll:

ROW 2: 1 sc into each of the first 7 ch, 1 hdc into each of the next 2 ch, 1 dc into each of the next 6 ch, 1 hdc into each of the next 2 ch, 1 sc into the last 7 ch. Sl st to close, and fasten off leaving a tail for sewing that is at least 3 times the length of the leaf.

LACY TRIM

To make the lacy trim, work rows of random open crochet sts along the lower edge of your garment. Create stitches of different heights (sc, hdc, dc and tr), either individually or in small groupings such as clusters and bobbles. Add crochet ch sts between the individual stitches or groupings. The more ch you add, the lacier your work will be.

Lay the work flat after every few sts to check that your freeform sts are going according to plan.

Working too many sts too close together will cause the border to flare out. Not working enough sts, or placing your sts too far apart, will cause the work to pucker. If the last st in any group is leaning backward, be sure to work sufficient sts soon after to bring the row back into alignment. If the final st in any group is leaning over toward the direction you are heading in, be sure to skip enough sts soon after so that the lace border stays relatively flat.

ASSEMBLY

Using the photographs of the finished garment as a guide, arrange the leaves over your completed garment and pin into place. Stitch neatly down the center of each leaf from the RS of the work. Before finishing the yarn off, pull on the seam gently to stretch the sts slightly and add a little ease. This will help to ensure that the stitching does not interfere with the drape of the garment.

FINISHING

When you have completed the lower border, firm and neaten up the edges of the knitting by working 1 row of sc sts right around the

garment, and then follow this with 1 row of crab st (see page 115 for step-by-step instructions on how to crochet a crab stitch). Again keep an eye on your stitches to ensure that you do not work too many or too few. Each sc st worked should stand perpendicular to the edge of the garment. If the sts begin to lean either forwards or backwards, pull the work back and adjust the number of sts being used before you proceed too far.

Work 1 rnd of sc foll by 1 rnd of crab st around each of the armholes. Weave in ends.

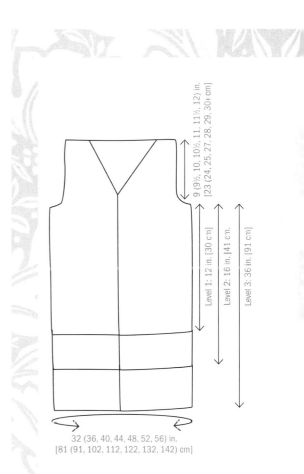

9 (9½, 10, 10½, 11, 11½, 12) in. [23 (24, 25, 27, 28, 29, 30 cm]

Level 1: 12 in. [30 cm]

Level 2: 16 in. [41 cm]

Level 3: 36 in. [91 cm]

32 (36, 40, 44, 48, 52, 56) in. [81 (91, 102, 112, 122, 132, 142) cm]

Elegante

The Spanish would call this vest *elegante* for its elegant leaves in beautiful colors. Our vest from *Level 1* becomes longer and more graceful with more than seventy leaves worked in various sizes and colors. Again, it's finished with a completely freeform lace trim. We've used one solid color and one similar, complementary variegated color. By now, you have some experience with freeform, too. So, if you've found other motifs, stitches or embellishments in other projects that you enjoyed making, add them here, too. Our garment is meant to give you ideas. Let your creativity be your guide.

Level **2**

BACK

Following the pattern on page 53, work as for Level 1 until piece measures 16" (41cm) from beg, ending with a WS row. Complete as for Level 1 from armhole shaping to shoulder.

LEFT FRONT

Work as for Level 1 until piece measures 16" (41cm) from beg, ending with a WS row. Complete as for Level 1 from armhole shaping to shoulder.

RIGHT FRONT

Work as for left front, reversing shaping.

FINISHING

Work as for Level 1.

FREEFORM EMBELLISHMENTS

SMALL LEAF

Work 20 small leaves, 25 medium leaves and 30 large leaves, just as for Level 1 (see page 55). Attach the leaves just as for Level 1.

LACY TRIM

Work as for Level 1, but make your lace a bit longer, and perhaps a little more complex. You might even consider using a color different from the vest. What do you envision? Remember to add bobbles, chs and other little interesting crochet sts to make your lace even more tactile. More chs will create an openwork look or you can use fewer chs between sts for a denser design. There are no rules. The most important part is to watch the final length and decide whether you want your border fairly even all the way around your vest. Work sc and crab st around the edges as for Level 1. Weave in ends.

Cosi va Bene

"That's just beautiful!" they'll shout in Italian. The words are as graceful as this long, silky vest. Regardless of your body shape, a long vest can enhance your figure and forgive those flaws we all have. Wear it with confidence and show off your beautiful freeform. Once again, our garment is merely an example of what can be done. Play with color and make this your own. We chose a palette of variegated yarn to give the illusion of far more colors than we actually used. The result is a wild and playful vest perfect for any occasion. Embrace the different sizes and shapes of your leaves to create this freeform treasure.

Tip

Try on the vest and check the length with your favorite shoes before adding the lacy trim. Jonelle got carried away and she has to wear stilettos when she wears her vest. She laughingly confesses that she was having so much fun making the lace trim that she forgot how short she is!

Note: Since this vest is considerably longer than the other 2 levels, you'll need additional yarn. See the materials list on page 53 for specific yarn amounts.

BACK

Following the pattern on page 53, work as for Level 1 until piece measures 36" (91cm) from beg, ending with a WS row. Complete as for Level 1 from armhole shaping to shoulder.

LEFT FRONT

Work as for Level 1 until piece measures 36" (91cm) from beg, ending with a WS row. Complete as for Level 1 from armhole shaping to shoulder.

RIGHT FRONT

Work as for left front, reversing shaping.

FINISHING

Work as for Level 1.

FREEFORM EMBELLISHMENTS

Our longest vest became a work of art adorned with many leaves in assorted sizes and colors. This is your chance to have fun and decorate your vest with style. Whether randomly or precisely placed, your leaves will add a fabulous design element to this stunning vest. Make all of the leaves you can imagine using, and arrange them all around the vest. Then...add even more. Have fun creating this amazing garment for your wardrobe.

SMALL LEAF

Make 30 or more small leaves, 35 or more medium leaves and 40 or more large leaves, just as for Level 1 (see page 55). Attach the embellishments just as for Level 1.

LACY TRIM

Work as for Level 1, making trim as elaborate as desired. Work sc and crab st around edges as for Level 1 (see page 115 for step-by-step instructions on how to crochet a crab stitch). Weave in ends.

Starfish Sweaters

At first glance this project takes a plain knitted shell top and overlays a fantastic freeform piece, transforming the garment into a wonderful, colorful garment. Each level adds more color, more freeform pieces, and more ideas to make it your own. We've used a simple starfish motif in our project. Any motif you have learned and enjoyed can be adapted to this garment. Now you are really embracing freeform. Another idea…jazz up a plain fabric tee shirt by creating a freeform "sheath" that lies over your basic shirt and gives you a wonderful and dressy new look. The possibilities are boundless.

Project Basics

Basic information for each level can be found with the rest of the level's instructions.

Schematics for sweaters on pages 61, 63, 65

Naturalis

Naturalis is Latin for natural, reflecting the wonderful star motif that adorns this simple and comfortable tee shirt. The tee is knit in a bamboo and cotton yarn dyed in rich, earthy colors. The resulting fabric is easy to wear and comfortable in all climates. Here we've transformed a very simple basic tee pattern into a captivating top, simply by adding an interesting overlay. Prudence also added unusual crochet detailing to the hem using spike stitches. Watch out here…crocheting these little stars is quite addictive!

SIZES
Women's XS (S, M, L, XL, 2X, 3X)

FINISHED MEASUREMENTS
Bust: 32 (36, 40, 44, 48, 52, 56)" (81 [91, 102, 112, 122, 132, 142]cm)

Length: 20½ (21½, 22½, 23½, 24½, 25½, 26½)" (52 [55, 57, 60, 62, 65, 67]cm)

YARN
7 (8, 9, 10, 11, 12, 12) skeins SWTC Terra, (bamboo/cotton blend, 120 yds [110m] per 50g skein) (A)

1 skein SWTC Terra, (bamboo/cotton blend, 120 yds [110m] per 50g skein) in each of 5 additional colors

NEEDLES AND HOOKS
US size 5 (3.75mm) 29" (74cm) circular needle

size E (3.5mm) crochet hook

NOTIONS
stitch markers
stitch holder
yarn needle

GAUGE
24 sts and 32 rows = 4" (10cm)

Level

1

BODY

With yarn A, CO 192 (216, 240, 264, 288, 312, 336) sts. Pm and join, being careful not to twist sts. Place second marker halfway across rnd to mark opposite side "seam." Work even in St st until piece measures 13 (13½, 14, 14½, 15, 15½, 16)" (33 [34, 36, 37, 38, 39, 41]cm) from beg.

DIVIDE FOR FRONT AND BACK

BO 6 (7, 8, 9, 10, 11, 12) sts. Work to next marker. Stop. Slip rem sts on holder. Turn. BO 6 (7, 8, 9, 10, 11, 12) sts. Complete row—84 (94, 104, 114, 124, 134, 144) sts for back.

BACK

Cont working these sts in St st until piece measures 20½ (21½, 22½, 23½, 24½, 25½, 26½)" (52 [55, 57, 60, 62, 65, 67]cm). BO across all sts.

FRONT

Place held sts on needle. Join yarn. With RS facing, work same as for back until piece measures 18 (19, 20, 21, 22, 23, 24)" (46 [48, 51, 53, 56, 58, 61]cm), ending with a WS row.

NECK SHAPING

NEXT ROW (RS): Work to center 12 (14, 16, 18, 20, 22, 24) sts, attach another ball of yarn, BO center 12 (14, 16, 18, 20, 22, 24) sts, complete row. Working both sides at once, BO 2 sts at each neck edge 3 times. Dec 1 st at each neck edge every row 7 (8, 9, 10, 11, 12, 13) times— 23 (26, 29, 32, 35, 38, 41) sts each side.

Work even until piece measures same as for back. BO rem shoulder sts.

FINISHING

Seam each shoulder. Work a rnd of sc and a rnd of crab st around the neck in yarn A and around armholes in a contrast color. Weave in ends.

FREEFORM EMBELLISHMENTS

Joining unique freeform embellishments as each is completed sometimes makes it difficult to achieve a good fit. However, stitching every single motif individually makes for quite a bit of extra work. We suggest a happy medium! Join some of the stars tog as you work to create short strips of 2 or more, or make small manageable groupings of 3 or 4 motifs.

To join motifs, carefully slip the hook from the ch at the top point of the arm, place the hook through the top st on the arm on the other motif, pick up the live st once again and cont on with the patt (see page 112 for step-by-step instructions on connecting the starfish).

The freeform embellishment on our Naturalis has 8 individual motifs, 8 strips of 2, plus 2 groups of 3. We invite you to use these numbers as guidelines. Making your basic knitted tee in a larger or smaller size will change the number of stars needed for your embellishment, as will covering more or less of the garment. Remember, there are no rules! Show your own personal style here.

SINGLE COLOR STAR (MAKE APPROXIMATELY 30)

Ch 3 and join with sl st to form a ring (see page 111 for step-by-step instructions on creating a starfish).

RND 1: Ch 3 (counts as first dc), work 11 dc into the ring and join with sl st to close the rnd—12 dc.

RND 2: *Ch 7, skip the first ch and work 1 sc into each of the next 2 ch, 1 hdc into each of the next 2 ch, 1 dc into each of the next 2 ch. Work 1 sc into each of the next 2 sts (these will be dc sts in the central circle). Rep from * 5 more times (6 "arms" total). Join with slip st to close, and fasten off.

ASSEMBLY

Once you have completed a good variety of motifs, individually and in groups and strips, arrange some of the stars over one side of your completed basic tee. Move them around until you are happy with the way all of the motifs fit tog. Pin the pieces tog wherever any of the points touch, and then neatly stitch using a yarn needle. Each time you stitch, choose a color that matches one of the outside rnds of crochet.

If you find you have some areas where the motifs do not quite come tog, create and add extra random "arms" or other small areas of crochet where needed. Weave in ends.

FINISHING

Instead of just working around the hem in sc, we added the occasional spike st approx every 4 or 5 sts in a contrast yarn, but you may work yours even more randomly.

To make a spike st, place the hook a few rows further down into the knitting, instead of just into the edge st. Make some of the spikes longer than others by sometimes placing the hook farther away from the edge. Each elongated st is made in a similar manner to a regular sc, except that after the initial wrap, you draw the yarn through far enough before the second wrap to prevent the edge from puckering—unless, of course, you would like to add a scalloped effect by gathering up the sts more tightly on the hem on your garment! Again, the choice is all yours. To complete the edging, add another rnd or 2 of sc sts, followed by a final rnd of crab st. Weave in ends.

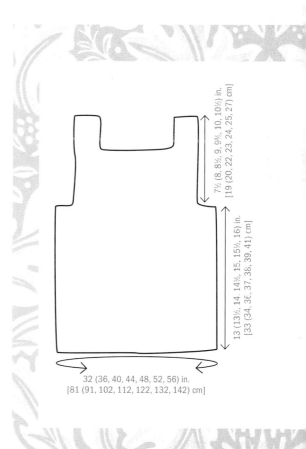

7½ (8, 8½, 9, 9½, 10, 10½) in. [19 (20, 22, 23, 24, 25, 27) cm]

13 (13½, 14, 14½, 15, 15½, 16) in. [33 (34, 36, 37, 38, 39, 41) cm]

32 (36, 40, 44, 48, 52, 56) in. [81 (91, 102, 112, 122, 132, 142) cm]

Étoile de Mer

We used the French translation of starfish to name our next project. *Étoile de Mer* brings color to our motifs. In this project, we'll add more starfish placed randomly to create a sheath effect over our simple tee. You can sprinkle stars in any manner. Create a sheath or just use your beautifully colored starfish to dress up your tee.

Level **2**

SIZES

Women's XS (S, M, L, XL, 2X, 3X)

FINISHED MEASUREMENTS

Bust: 32 (36, 40, 44, 48, 52, 56)" (81 [91, 102, 112, 122, 132, 142]cm)

Length: 25½ (26½, 27½, 28½, 29½, 30½, 31½)" (65 [67, 70, 72, 75, 77, 80]cm)

YARN

11 (12, 13, 14, 15, 16, 17) skeins SWTC Terra, (bamboo/cotton blend, 120 yds [110m] per 50g skein) (A)

1 skein SWTC Terra, (bamboo/cotton blend, 120 yds [110m] per 50g skein) in each of 7 additional colors

NEEDLES AND HOOKS

US size 5 (3.75mm) 29" (74cm) circular needle

size E (3.5mm) crochet hook

NOTIONS

stitch markers
stitch holder
yarn needle

GAUGE

24 sts and 32 rows = 4" (10cm)

FRONT

Following the pattern on page 61, with yarn A, work as for Level 1 until piece measures 18 (18½, 19, 19½, 20, 20½, 21)" (46 [47, 48, 50, 51, 52, 53]cm) from beg. Then divide the front and back and cont to work as for Level 1 until piece measures 23 (24, 25, 26, 27, 28, 29)" (58 [61, 64, 66, 69, 71, 74]cm), ending with a WS row.

BACK

Work as for Level 1 until piece measures 25½ (26½, 27½, 28½, 29½, 30½, 31½)" (65 [67, 70, 72, 75, 77, 80]cm). BO across all sts. Then work the neck shaping as for Level 1.

SLEEVES (MAKE 2)

With yarn A, CO 72 (78, 84, 90, 96, 102, 108) sts. Work even for 2" (5cm) in St st (if desired,

begin with 1" (3cm) cuff in k1, p1 rib). Inc 1 st at each end (with M1) every other row 9 times—90 (96, 102, 108, 114, 120, 126) sts.

Work even until piece measures 6" (15cm). BO.

FINISHING

Seam each shoulder. Sew in sleeves.

To finish the neck and bottom edges, work a rnd of sc and a rnd of crab st around. Weave in ends.

FREEFORM EMBELLISHMENTS

To join motifs, carefully slip the hook from the ch at the top point of the arm, place the hook through the top st on the arm on the other motif, pick up the live st once again, and cont on with the patt.

When creating the 2-color star motifs, avoid putting colors that are very close in tone or intensity tog unless you want the colors to merge. Also avoid using the same color as your base garment for any of the outside rnds of crochet as this will cause such motifs to disappear into the background.

Our *Étoile de Mer* version was made by stitching tog 20 individual motifs, 10 strips of 2 and 12 groups of 3 motifs.

2-COLOR STAR (MAKE APPROXIMATELY 76 MOTIFS)

Work as for single-color star, but use a different color for each rnd (see page 61).

ASSEMBLY

Work as for Level 1.

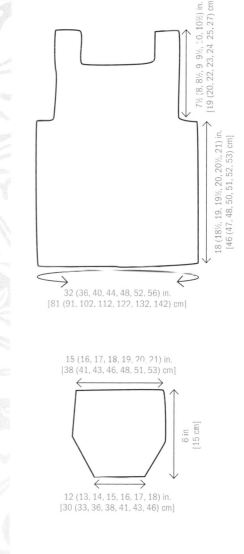

7½ (8, 8½, 9, 9½, 10, 10½) in. [19 (20, 22, 23, 24, 25, 27) cm]

18 (18½, 19, 19½, 20, 20½, 21) in. [46 (47, 48, 50, 51, 52, 53) cm]

32 (36, 40, 44, 48, 52, 56) in. [81 (91, 102, 112, 122, 132, 142) cm]

15 (16, 17, 18, 19, 20, 21) in. [38 (41, 43, 46, 48, 51, 53) cm]

6 in [15 cm]

12 (13, 14, 15, 16, 17, 18) in. [30 (33, 36, 38, 41, 43, 46) cm]

Flor do Mar

OK, so is it really a starfish or is it more of a star flower? That's the neat thing about freeform—it can be anything you want! We debated it too and couldn't decide, so we named this garment *Flor do Mar*, the Portuguese phrase for sea flower. *Flor do Mar* uses our simple tee pattern again and showcases yarn in eight different colors. Prudence went wild with star flowers in many different color combinations. The fascinating necklace effect of the starfish neckline makes this top a real standout.

Level
3

SIZES

Women's XS (S, M, L, XL, 2X, 3X)

FINISHED MEASUREMENTS

Bust: 32 (36, 40, 44, 48, 52, 56)" (81 [91, 102, 112, 122, 132, 142]cm)

Length: 20½ (21½, 22½, 23½, 24½, 25½, 26½)" (52 [55, 57, 60, 62, 65, 67]cm)

YARN

9 (10, 11, 12, 13, 14, 15) skeins SWTC Terra, (bamboo/cotton blend, 120 yds [110m] per 50g skein) (A)

1 skein SWTC Terra, (bamboo/cotton blend, 120 yds [110m] per 50g skein) in each of 7 additional colors

NEEDLES AND HOOKS

US size 5 (3.75mm) 29" (74cm) circular needle

size E (3.5mm) crochet hook

NOTIONS

stitch markers
stitch holder
yarn needle

GAUGE

24 sts and 32 rows = 4" (10cm)

Following pattern on page 63, work as for Level 2, dividing for front and back when piece measures 13 (13½, 14, 14½, 15, 15½, 16)" (33 [34, 36, 37, 38, 39, 41]cm) from beg.

FREEFORM EMBELLISHMENTS

We're going to make a lot of starfish for this beauty! In our *Flor do Mar* version there are 22 individual stars and 10 sets of 3 stars, tog with 2 long strips for the bottom borders, each of which contains 8 joined stars. Use these numbers as guidelines only. Again, making your basic knitted tee in a larger or smaller size will change the number of stars needed for your embellishment, as will covering more or less of the garment. Remember that the tee is just a blank canvas here. It is an opportunity to place the stars either totally randomly or more precisely—whichever way you feel will create the most interesting

shape for your sheath. Stitch or tie some of the stars into place, especially at the edges of the design, so that the top stays positioned the way you envision and is less fussy to wear.

To join some of the motifs into sets or strips, carefully slip the hook from the ch at the top point of the arm, place the hook through the top st on the arm on the other motif, pick up the live st once again and cont with the patt (see page 112 for step-by-step instructions on connecting the starfish).

2-COLOR STAR (MAKE APPROXIMATELY 68 MOTIFS OR MORE)

Work as for Level 2 (see page 63).

ASSEMBLY

Work as for Level 1.

To suspend the crochet motifs from the neck in this version, place the stars in position starting approx 1" to 2" (3cm to 5cm) from the neck edge. Pin them into place, and then create additional arms around the neck edge where they are needed to join the stars onto the border. Slip the top ch of the new arm through the point of the relevant star, as described earlier, or stitch the points tog.

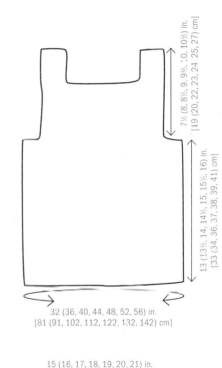

7½ (8, 8½, 9, 9½, 10, 10½) in. [19 (20, 22, 23, 24, 25, 27) cm]

13 (13½, 14, 14½, 15, 15½, 16) in. [33 (34, 36, 37, 38, 39, 41) cm]

32 (36, 40, 44, 48, 52, 56) in. [81 (91, 102, 112, 122, 132, 142) cm]

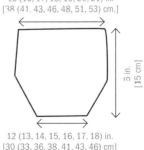

15 (16, 17, 18, 19, 20, 21) in. [38 (41, 43, 46, 48, 51, 53) cm.]

5 in. [15 cm]

12 (13, 14, 15, 16, 17, 18) in. [30 (33, 36, 38, 41, 43, 46) cm]

Basic Tees

In freeform, a basic tee is merely a canvas for extraordinary artistry!

This project shows you that every project can become a glamor garment that will make you stand out in a crowd. Here, Prudence took Jonelle's basic tee shirt pattern, boring by her own admission, and transformed the design into two glamorous evening tops, and in *Level 3*, a show-stopping evening dress.

SWTC's Yin and Yang yarns provided the elegant palette, and the seductive sequins that draw your eye to this stunning project. Watch how these knit leaves combine with simple surface crochet to capture your imagination and make this project truly spectacular.

Project Basics

Basic information including the pattern for each level can be found with the rest of the level's instructions.

Schematics for Basic Tee on pages 69, 71, 73

Scintilla

We've chosen the Italian word *scintilla*, which means sparkle, for this project. We've used sequined yarn to take a very simple knit shell and turn it into an extraordinary sparkling beauty. *Scintilla* defines the magic of freeform!

In previous projects, we learned how to make small, simple leaves. In *Scintilla*, the leaves become much larger, with a bit of added bling and dazzle. You'll also learn how to make a zigzag border that can be added to any straight-edge sweater to really jazz it up. Finally, Prudence offers a new finish for neck and armhole edges with her provocative neckline featuring a garter stitch border.

Level
1

SIZES
Women's XS (S, M, L, XL, 2X, 3X)

FINISHED MEASUREMENTS
Bust: 32 (36, 40, 44, 48, 52, 56)" (81 [91, 102, 112, 122, 132, 142]cm)
Length: 15½ (16½, 17½, 18½, 19½, 20½, 21½)" (39 [42, 44, 47, 50, 52, 55]cm)

YARN
4 (5, 6, 7, 8, 9, 10) skeins SWTC Yin (wool/silk/bamboo blend, 164 yds [150m] per 50g skein) (A)

1 skein SWTC Yang (wool/silk/bamboo blend with sequins, 110 yds [100m] per 50g skein) (B)

NEEDLES AND HOOKS
US size 6 (4mm) straight and 16" (41cm) circular needles

NOTIONS
stitch markers

stitch holder

yarn needle

GAUGE
20 sts and 27 rows= 4" (10cm) in St st

BACK

With yarn A, CO 80 (90, 100, 110, 120, 130, 140) sts. Work in St st until piece measures 8 (8½, 9, 9½, 10, 10½, 11)" (20 [22, 23, 24, 25, 27, 28]cm), ending with a WS row. Mark last row on each side for armholes.

SLEEVE SHAPING

Inc 1 st each armhole edge every RS row 3 times, then every 6th row 7 times—100 (110, 120, 130, 140, 150, 160) sts.

Work even until armhole measures 7½ (8, 8½, 9, 9½, 10, 10½)" (19 [20, 22, 23, 24, 25, 27] cm), ending with a WS row.

NECK AND SHOULDER SHAPING

NEXT ROW (RS): Knit to center 36 (38, 40, 42, 44, 46, 48) sts, join a second ball of yarn, BO center 36 (38, 40, 42, 44, 46, 48) sts, work to end—32 (36, 40, 44, 48, 52, 56) sts each side.

Working both sides at once, BO 6 sts at each neck edge 3 times—18 (20, 22, 26, 30, 34, 38) sts each side. BO.

FRONT

Work as for back until armhole measures 3" (8cm) less than back.

NECK AND SHOULDER SHAPING

Knit to center 40 (42, 44, 46, 48, 50, 52) sts, join a second ball of yarn, BO center 40 (42, 44, 46, 48, 50, 52) sts, work to end. Cont to work sleeve inc, dec 1 st at neck edge every row 12 (14, 16, 16, 16, 16, 16) times—18 (20, 22, 26, 30, 34, 38) sts.

Work until piece measures same as back. BO.

FINISHING

Sew shoulder and side seams from hem to markers. Weave in ends.

NECK AND ARMHOLE TRIM

With yarn B and circular needle, pick up 3 out of every 4 sts around neck and shoulder openings. Join in a rnd. Work in garter st for ½" (1cm). BO loosely. (Alternately, work 1 rnd of sc, then 1 rnd of crab st.)

FREEFORM EMBELLISHMENTS

Our Level 1 design has a randomly knitted freeform border stitched to the lower edge, and just a few knitted leaves gently draping from the right shoulder. Here are some directions to guide you:

When making the freeform additions, choose tools that give you the look and feel you desire. If, like us, you wish the embellishments to drape softly, use slightly larger needles and hooks than those used for the body of the garment. The larger the needles or hook, the looser and softer your sts.

RANDOM ZIGZAG BORDER

Using the yarn of your choice (Yin or Yang), CO approx 5 sts and knit 1 row. Working in garter st, make random inc or dec in most rows, but only at 1 edge of the border. The number of sts in our border ranged between 5 and 10 sts, but you can make your edging narrower or deeper if desired. Cont knitting and shaping 1 edge of your piece until it fits around the hem of the completed garment. BO and stitch the border neatly into position.

GARTER STITCH LEAVES (MAKE AS DESIRED)

CO 2 or 3 sts and knit 2 or 3 rows. Using any method of inc, create an extra st in the next row (this can be done at the beg, end or middle of the row). Work a few more rows without any shaping, and then inc again somewhere along the next row. Do not inc every row, or your piece will become more like a triangle than a leaf. Instead, make your inc whenever you feel that they are needed to create a pleasing "leaflike" shape. Once any motif is the desired width, work 1" to 2" (3cm to 5cm) straight, with no further shaping. Then either bind off (for a straight top), or begin to slowly and randomly dec the sts back down towards a point again (for a fully formed leaf shape).

CROCHET CHAIN EMBELLISHMENT

Embellish the leaves, particularly any plainer ones that have been knit in Yin, by adding crochet ch sts to create veins, as foll:

Hold B at the back of the work, and the crochet hook at the front, and pull through a loop of yarn at 1 end of the leaf. Place the hook down though the knitting once again, at the position where you wish the next st to be. Wrap yarn around hook, and pull the new loop through the knitting, and at the same time, through the loop on the hook. Cont making sts in this manner to create a central vein down the leaf, and then fasten off at the other end. For added visual interest, create a number of smaller, separate veins branching out from the central line of crochet, especially on the larger motifs. (See pages 118–119 for step-by-step instructions on crocheting through knitted fabric.)

ASSEMBLY

Make as many leaves as you wish. Arrange them on your garment, pin them and stitch neatly in place. Weave in ends.

7½ (8, 8½, 9, 9½, 10, 10½) in.
[19 (20, 22, 23, 24, 25, 27) cm]

8 (8½, 9, 9½, 10, 10½, 11) in.
[20 (22, 23, 24, 25, 27, 28) cm]

32 (36, 40, 44, 48, 52, 56) in.
[81 (91, 102, 112, 122, 132, 142) cm]

Izleses

A friend in Hungary called this tee *Izleses*, a word that referred to its tasteful elegance. The glamorous leaves are a spectacular finish for the neck. The tapered bottom edge is merely an illusion created by the placement and length of individual leaves. The result is a slimming effect as your eye notices all of the interesting shapes and subtle details. Plan the leaf placement to create your own interesting finishing touches. The number of leaves you will need depends on the size, length and placement of your finished pieces. Again, there is no set formula and no rules. You can also add knitted or crocheted bobbles randomly on the leaves, and work in more sparkling veins on individual leaves to make this garment a standout. Use our example to guide your placement and turn to your inner artist to dictate your final, exquisite piece.

Level
2

SIZES

Women's XS (S, M, L, XL, 2X, 3X)

FINISHED MEASUREMENTS

Bust: 32 (36, 40, 44, 48, 52, 56)" (81 [91, 102, 112, 122, 132, 142]cm)

Length: 17½ (18½, 19½, 20½, 21½, 22½, 23½)" (44 [47, 50, 52, 55, 57, 60]cm)

YARN

5 (6, 7, 8, 9, 10, 11) skeins SWTC Yin (wool/ silk/bamboo blend, 164 yds [150m] per 50g skein) (A)

2 skeins SWTC Yang (wool/silk/bamboo blend with sequins, 110 yds [100m] per 50g skein) (B)

NEEDLES AND HOOKS

US size 6 (4mm) straight and 16" (41cm) circular needles

NOTIONS

stitch markers
stitch holder
yarn needle

GAUGE

20 sts and 27 rows = 4" (10cm) in St st

Follow the pattern beginning on page 69 to knit the top, working the sleeve shaping when piece measures 10 (10½, 11, 11½, 12, 12½, 13)" (25 [27, 28, 29, 30, 32, 33]cm).

FREEFORM EMBELLISHMENTS

GARTER STITCH LEAVES
(MAKE AS DESIRED)

Work the garter st leaves as for Level 1. Unless you wish your leaves to curl at the edges, choose a st patt that lays flat. We used garter st for our examples, but you could try working some of the leaves in seed st or 1" x 1" (3cm x 3cm) rib for a little more variety!

CROCHET CHAIN EMBELLISHMENT

Work the crochet ch embellishment on the leaves as for Level 1. For the most organic look, do not work these chain sts in straight lines, but allow them to wind their way softly over the piece in a "natural" fashion. (See pages 118–119 for step-by-step instructions on crocheting through knitted fabric.)

BOBBLES

If desired, you may also randomly add small knit or crochet bobbles. Leave a yarn tail about 4" (10cm) long at each end of the bobble to tie it into place or stitch it down.

KNITTED BOBBLES: CO 1 st, knit in the front and back of this st until there are 5 sts. Knit 5 rows, then knit all sts tog in the next row. Fasten off.

CROCHETED BOBBLES: Ch 3, *yo, place the hook into the sl st, yo and pull through, yo again and pull through the first 2 loops on the hook. Rep from * approx 3 more times, then work a final yo and pull it through all the loops on the hook. Fasten off.

ASSEMBLY

Arrange the leaves on your garment. In our *Izleses*, we have used leaves to finish the neck and lower trim. Pin your leaves into place, and try the garment on to make sure they lay appropriately. Once you are satisfied, sew them neatly into place.

If desired, make a random row of additional crochet ch sts above the line of leaves at the hem to create a visual balance between the main garment and the added embellishments. Use the photos of our Level 2 garment as a guide.

Arrange the bobbles on the leaves and tie or stitch them in place to help to hold the leaves in position and also to create additional texture and interest. Weave in ends.

7½ (8, 8½, 9, 9½, 10, 10½) in.
[19 (20, 22, 23, 24, 25, 27) cm.]

20 (10½, 11, 11½, 12, 12½, 13) in.
[25 (27, 28, 29, 30, 32, 33) cm.]

32 (36, 40, 44, 48, 52, 56) in.
[81 (91, 102, 112, 122, 132, 142) cm.]

Nyskabende

We named this version *Nyskabende*, a tribute in Danish to the "innovative design" of this next project. When we finished this dress, we both sat back in awe of how gorgeous freeform could be. Now that you have tackled the basic knitted leaves, crochet chain surface work and bobbles of various types, you can follow the same basic pattern from *Levels 1* and *2* to knit a dress. Watch how the same simple techniques transform a very plain dress pattern into a showstopper. Instead of knitting plain leaves and adding the bling with surface work, let's make the leaves sparkle from the start and knit them solely from sequined yarn. Then in this example we'll use that crochet chain stitch to create a playful and random finish around the neck and again above the hemline. Scatter those fun little bobbles wherever you'd like, and you'll have the most magnificent garment!

Level
3

SIZES
Women's XS (S, M, L, XL, 2X, 3X)

FINISHED MEASUREMENTS
Bust: 32 (36, 40, 44, 48, 52, 56)" (81 [91, 102, 112, 122, 132, 142]cm)
Length: 28½ (29½, 30½, 31½, 32½, 33½, 34½)" (72 [75, 77, 80, 83, 85, 88]cm)

YARN
8 (9, 10, 11, 12, 13, 14) skeins SWTC Yin (wool/silk/bamboo blend, 164 yds [150m] per 50g skein) (A)

3 skeins SWTC Yang (wool/silk/bamboo blend with sequins, 110 yds [100m] per 50g skein) (B)

NEEDLES AND HOOKS
US size 6 (4mm) straight and 16" (41cm) circular needles

NOTIONS
stitch markers
stitch holder
yarn needle

GAUGE
20 sts and 27 rows = 4" (10cm) in St st

To make the dress, work as for Level 1 (see page 69), working sleeve shaping when piece measures 21 (21½, 22, 22½, 23, 23½, 24)" (53 [55, 56, 57, 58, 60, 61]cm). The dress is worked exactly the same as the top, only longer.

FREEFORM EMBELLISHMENTS

GARTER STITCH LEAVES
Work the garter st leaves as for Level 1. Embellish the leaves with crochet chs as for levels 1 and 2, if desired.

CROCHET CHAIN EMBELLISHMENT
Now work additional areas of crochet onto the surface of the garment in any pattern you like. Always keep a careful eye on the work, and check after every few chs to be sure you are happy with how the random stc are progressing. If the sts appear a little too tight, or if they are not travelling in a totally pleasing path, pull out the last few sts and try again. Consider adding swirls of crochet in B to the hemline, just above

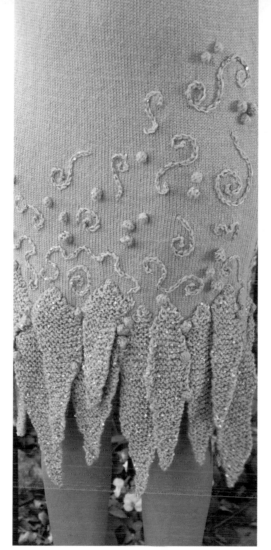

the leaves, or more randomly anywhere on the garment. This type of embollishment will also look fabulous around the neck, drawing attention back to the top of your garment. (See pages 118–119 for step-by-step instructions on crocheting through knit fabric.)

Once you have completed the ch stitching, randomly add bobbles to help balance your design. (See the pattern on page 109 for instructions on making bobbles.) Use the photo of our Level 3 *Nyskabende* for inspiration on where to place the bobbloc. Weave in ends.

A-Line Skirts

Pert and pretty describes these bamboo skirts. Straight knit (or crochet) panels in SWTC Bamboo are finished with an elastic waist to make a simple skirt. Adjust the length to suit your own style. With a new twist on fringe, the simple skirts become extraordinary. The easily made fringe offers us the chance to embellish and create the illusion of a tapered edge on the skirt. Make sure to check out the unusual belts too. Your own freeform style will guide you in creating a belt using your favorite stitches and motifs. Try it. We know you can make something special.

Project Basics

SIZES
Women's XS (S, M, L, XL, 2X, 3X)

FINISHED MEASUREMENTS
Waist: 24 (28, 32, 34, 36, 38, 40)" (61 [71, 81, 86, 91, 97, 102]cm)

Hips: 32 (36, 40, 44, 48, 52, 56)" (81 [91, 102, 112, 122, 132, 142]cm)

Length: 21" (53cm)

YARN
All levels:
5 (5, 6, 7, 8, 9, 10) skeins SWTC Bamboo (100% bamboo, 250 yds [228m] per 100g skein)

Level 3:
Additional skeins of SWTC Bamboo in contrasting colors, if desired

NEEDLES AND HOOKS
All levels:
US size 4 (3.5mm) needles
US size 6 (4mm) needles
size F (3.75mm) crochet hook (optional)

NOTIONS
1" (3cm) wide elastic, length to match waist measurement

2 large stitch holders (or yarn/string), each long enough to hold all sts from 1 panel

sewing needle and thread

yarn needle

GAUGE
24 sts and 32 rows = 4" (10cm) in St st using smaller needles

Schematic for A-Line Skirt on page 77

Adornado

Adornado is the Spanish word for ornate, a word that aptly describes our first wonderful bamboo skirt. We've made a simple, A-line skirt look fantastic with fabulous fringing. The skirt is handknit here, but if you have a knitting machine you can cheat and get it done faster! The fringe gives *Adornado* an asymmetrical look as it moves from knee length on one side to long, flowing fringe on the other. Watch how it swishes as you walk.

Level
1

FRONT AND BACK (MAKE 2)

With larger needles, CO 192 (220, 240, 264, 288, 312, 336) sts.

NEXT ROW (WS): * P1, k1; rep from * across.

Work in St st for 3" (8cm).

On next RS row, change to smaller needles and k2tog across row—96 (110, 120, 132, 144, 156, 168) sts.

Work even in St st until skirt measures 17" (43cm) from beg or desired length, ending with a WS row.

NEXT (DEC) Row (RS): K1, ssk, knit to last 3 sts, k2tog, k1.

Rep dec row every 4th row a total of 4 times—88 (102, 112, 124, 136, 148, 160) sts.

Work even in St st until skirt measures 20" (51cm), ending with a WS row.

WAISTBAND

Change to larger needles.

NEXT ROW (RS): *K2, k2tog; rep across row, ending with K2 on size S only—66 (77, 84, 93, 102, 111, 120) sts.

Work even in St st for 2" (5cm). Place sts on a holder.

FINISHING

Sew side seams. With sewing needle and thread, firmly sew ends of elastic tog so they are 2" (5cm) smaller than waist measurement, overlapping ends. With yarn needle, sew live sts from holder to first row of waistband, sandwiching elastic between. Weave in ends.

FREEFORM EMBELLISHMENTS

If you had fun making the fringe on our bamboo purses (see pages 46 through 51), you will really enjoy this project. This skirt needs a lot of fringe.

Make the fringe by knitting or crocheting. The effect will be similar in either case. There are instructions for both techniques, but if you are equally proficient at both crafts you will probably find crocheting faster.

FRINGE (MAKE 200 OR MORE IN VARYING LENGTHS)

KNIT METHOD: With smaller needles, CO the desired number of sts. Knit 1 row. BO.

CROCHET METHOD: With crochet hook, ch the desired number of sts. Sc in 2nd ch from hook and each ch to end. Fasten off.

When cutting off the yarn, leave a tail long enough to tie or sew to the lower edge of the skirt. Or work a small bunch of fringe sections, as described below, before finishing off.

Work 20 fringe for each of the foll foundation row lengths (a total of 10 sections for the front and 10 for the back).

FOUNDATION ROW LENGTHS

CH 20 (if crocheting), or CO 20 (if knitting).
CH 23 (if crocheting), or CO 23 (if knitting).
CH 26 (if crocheting), or CO 26 (if knitting).
CH 29 (if crocheting), or CO 29 (if knitting).
CH 32 (if crocheting), or CO 32 (if knitting).
CH 35 (if crocheting), or CO 35 (if knitting).
CH 38 (if crocheting), or CO 38 (if knitting).
CH 41 (if crocheting), or CO 41 (if knitting).
CH 44 (if crocheting), or CO 44 (if knitting).
CH 47 (if crocheting), or CO 47 (if knitting).

For the larger sizes, cont to inc the starting lengths by 3 as foll, until you have sufficient sections of fringe to reach around your skirt:
CH 50 (if crocheting), or CO 50 (if knitting).
CH 53 (if crocheting), or CO 53 (if knitting).

ASSEMBLY

There are many different ways to work and attach the fringe. Ours were done in crochet and worked in small bunches, with 5 lengths of fringe per bunch. 2 bunches in each length were attached next to each other across the front of the skirt, and again on the back. They were then tied into place, with the ends woven in neatly at the back of the work. You might like to create your fringe in bunches in this manner, or perhaps you would prefer to make each length of fringe individually, and later tie or stitch them to the skirt. Or perhaps you would rather save yourself any extra finishing at all, by working your sts directly into the hem of the skirt, attaching the fringe as you go. Because this is freeform, choose

12 (14, 16, 17, 18, 19, 20) in.
[30 (36, 41, 43, 46, 48, 51) cm]

21 in.
[53 cm]

16 (18, 20, 22, 24, 26, 28) in.
[41 (46, 51, 56, 61, 66, 71) cm]

whichever method works best for you. Depending on the size of the garment and how closely you attach the embellishments, each skirt will require a total of approx 200 or more individual sections of fringe.

Arrange the lengths of fringe so that half of the pieces are attached in either ascending or descending order across the front of the skirt, with the other half across the back of the skirt to correspond.

Weave in ends.

BELT (OPTIONAL)

If you like, you can make a simple belt by either knitting or crocheting a straight strip to the desired length. Measure your waist and increase the measurement to allow for a tie length plus enough extra for tails to hang down from your tie. Knit in garter st by casting sts to the desired width (approx 3" [8cm]), and knitting to the desired length. BO.

The same effect can be achieved in crochet. Make a ch to the desired width and work rows of any height crochet st until the piece is the desired length. Fasten off. Consider adding some fringe to the ends of your belt to match your skirt.

Capriccioso

From Italian comes the name *capriccioso*, meaning whimsical. The basic skirt is used again with a delightful fringe worked to curl delicately at the ends. We've staggered the length of the ends here, too, and the random placement gives the skirt a flapper quality. This enchantingly playful bamboo skirt is captivating to wear. Adding a freeform belt is a great finishing touch!

Follow the pattern beginning on page 77 to knit the skirt. Then add freeform fringe embellishments as follows.

FREEFORM EMBELLISHMENTS

FRINGE (MAKE 200 OR MORE)

For *Capriccioso*, make more than 200 individual fringe pieces.

Make the fringe as for Level 1 (see page 77), but add some curl to the ends by binding off more tightly than normal in knit or tightening your tension in crochet (see page 122 for tips).

The sections of fringe in our example were crocheted. They were worked in bunches, with 4 sections of varying length to each bunch. Every bunch contained:

1 section worked on approx 15 ch

1 section worked on approx 22 ch

1 section worked on approx 30 ch

1 section worked on approx 36 ch

ASSEMBLY

As well as attaching the fringe to the hem of the skirt, using the method described in Level 1, make a few additional bunches and randomly add them elsewhere on the skirt. Weave in ends.

FREEFORM BELT (OPTIONAL)

Crochet a foundation ch, or CO a row of knitting to the desired length. Work rows of sc, or rows of garter st and create elongated, random "holes" in the work as often as you desire. To make these holes, occasionally either chain a few sts and then skip a corresponding number of sts before cont on, or BO a few sts and then, in the foll row, CO that number again over the gap. Attach a few lengths of fringe to the ends of the belt, if desired. Knit or crochet 2 small tabs as loops to keep the belt in place at the waist, and stitch them in place on the side seams of the skirt (see page 114 for step-by-step instructions for creating holes in a crochet belt).

Magique

The French word for magic became the name for our final bamboo skirt project. Here, we add three more colors and invite you to throw your creativity into making this fringe the focal point of your finished piece. *Magique* will be one of those treasured pieces in your wardrobe that can transition easily from office to evening.

Follow the pattern beginning on page 77 to knit the skirt. Then add freeform fringe embellishments as follows.

FREEFORM EMBELLISHMENTS

FRINGE (MAKE 200 OR MORE)

Make the fringe as for Level 1, in bunches of random lengths. In the Level 3 garment, although 5 different colors are used altogether, each bunch is worked in a single color. Each bunch contains 2 to 5 sections of fringe in varying lengths.

ASSEMBLY

Randomly arrange the sections of fringe around the hem of the garment, and tie or stitch into place.

FREEFORM BELT

Work as for Level 2, incorporating more colors as desired.

Level
3

Open Jackets

Our open jacket takes a classic, boxy sweater pattern and introduces a realm of possibilities. With some planning, you'll soon find that you can knit your favorite sweater pattern and skip the directions for the ribbing, cuffs, and neck line, substituting your own freeform magic. That's what we've done here. Simple knit patches combined with surface embroidery make this project a standout.

Project Basics

SIZES
Women's XS (S, M, L, XL, 2X, 3X)

FINISHED MEASUREMENTS
Bust: 32 (36, 40, 44, 48, 52, 56)" (81 [91, 102, 112, 122, 132, 142]cm)
Length: 20 (21, 22, 23, 24, 25, 26)" (51 [53, 56, 58, 61, 64, 66]cm)

YARN
All levels:
8 (8, 9, 10, 11, 12, 13) skeins SWTC Pure (Soysilk®, 164 yds [150m] per 50g skein) (A)

1 skein SWTC Pure (Soysilk®, 164 yds [150m] per 50g skein) in each of 3 or more additional colors, as desired

NEEDLES AND HOOKS
All levels:
US size 4 (3.5mm) and 16" (41cm) and 36" (91cm) circular needles

US size 5 (3.75mm) 36" (91cm) circular needle

size F (3.75mm) crochet hook

NOTIONS
stitch markers
stitch holders
yarn needle

GAUGE
22 sts and 30 rows = 4" (10cm) using larger needles

Schematic for Open Jacket on page 85

Vakker

Vakker is Norwegian for "beautiful," which is the perfect word to define another exquisite freeform project. Here, we will show you how to take a basic cardigan and turn it into pure beauty. In creating *Vakker*, we will knit the basic pieces of a cardigan and leave all of the finishing to our freeform work. The cuffs, neck and hem will all be finished with new techniques introduced in this open jacket. Check out the embroidery work! It is amazing how such a simple and often overlooked art can add so much to our knitted garment. Freeform combines many art forms to take a simple garment and make it a magical—and wearable—work of art.

Level
1

BODY

With yarn A and larger needles, CO 176 (196, 220, 240, 264, 284, 308) sts. Do not join. Work back and forth in St st until piece measures 12½ (13, 13½, 14, 14½, 15, 15½)" (32 [33, 34, 36, 37, 38, 39]cm) from beg, ending with a WS row.

DIVIDE FOR FRONT AND BACK

NEXT ROW (RS): K34 (39, 45, 48, 53, 56, 62) sts and place on holder for right front, BO 20 (20, 20, 24, 26, 30, 30) sts for right underarm, knit 68 (78, 90, 96, 106, 112, 124) sts for back, place rem 54 (59, 65, 72, 79, 86, 92) sts on holder for left underarm and front.

BACK

ARMHOLE SHAPING

Working on back sts only, dec 1 st each end every RS row 4 (4, 5, 5, 6, 7, 7) times—60 (70, 80, 86, 94, 98, 110) sts.

Work even until armhole measures 7½ (8, 8½, 9, 9½, 10, 10½)" (19 [20, 22, 23, 24, 25, 27]cm), ending with a WS row.

NECK AND SHOULDER SHAPING

Mark center 30 (32, 36, 38, 40, 44, 48) sts.

NEXT ROW (RS): Knit to first marker, join second ball of yarn and BO marked sts, knit to end of row. Working both sides at once, dec 1 st at each neck edge every row 3 times. AT THE SAME TIME, BO 5 (6, 8, 8, 10, 10, 11) sts at beg of next 2 rows, then BO 5 (7, 8, 9, 10, 10, 12) at beg of foll 2 rows, then BO 6 (7, 8, 9, 10, 11, 12) at beg of next 2 rows.

LEFT FRONT

Place held sts for left front on needle. With RS facing, join yarn at underarm.

BO 20 (20, 20, 24, 26, 30, 30) sts. Dec 1 st at armhole edge every RS row 4 (4, 5, 5, 6, 7, 7) times—30 (35, 40, 43, 47, 49, 55) sts.

Work even until armhole measures 4 (4½, 5, 5½, 6, 6½, 7)" (10 [11, 13, 14, 15, 17, 18]cm), ending with a RS row.

NECK SHAPING

NEXT ROW (WS): BO 9 (10, 11, 12, 12, 13, 15) sts, work to end of row. Dec 1 st at neck edge every RS row 5 times—16 (20, 24, 26, 30, 31, 35) sts.

Work even until armhole measures same as for back.

SHOULDER SHAPING

BO 5 (6, 8, 8, 10, 10, 11) sts at beg of next RS row, then BO 5 (7, 8, 9, 10, 10, 12) at beg of foll RS row, then BO 6 (7, 8, 9, 10, 11, 12) at beg of next RS row.

RIGHT FRONT

Work same as for left front from beg of armhole dec, reversing shaping.

SLEEVES

With yarn A and larger needles, CO 44 (46, 46, 50, 50, 56, 56) sts. Working in St st, inc 1 each end every 4th row 19 (21, 24, 25, 28, 28, 31) times—82 (88, 94, 100, 106, 112, 118) sts.

Work even until sleeve measures 17 (17½, 18, 18½, 18½, 19, 19)" (43 [44, 46, 47, 47, 48, 48]cm) from beg, ending with a WS row.

CAP SHAPING

BO 10 (10, 10, 12, 13, 15, 15) sts at beg of next 2 rows.

Dec 1 st each end every RS row 4 (4, 5, 5, 6, 7, 7) times—54 (60, 64, 66, 68, 68, 74) sts.

Dec 1 st each end every row 15 (15, 17, 17, 19, 19, 21) times—24 (30, 30, 32, 30, 30, 32) sts.

BO 3 sts at beg of next 4 rows—12 (18, 18, 20, 18, 18, 20) sts.

BO rem sts.

FINISHING

Sew shoulder seams. Sew sleeves into armholes. Sew sleeve and side seams. Weave in ends.

FREEFORM EMBELLISHMENTS

SLIP STITCH MOTIF (MAKE AS MANY AS DESIRED)

To begin, choose 2 contrasting colors.

Using color 1, CO the desired number of sts. It must be an odd number (samples were worked with 9 or 11 sts). Knit 1 foundation row.

PATTERN ROW 1 (RS): Using color 2 , *k1, then (still keeping the yarn at the back of the work) sl the next st purlwise. Rep from * to last st, k1.

PATTERN ROW 2: Using color 2, *p1, sl the next st purlwise. Rep from * to the end of the row.

PATTERN ROWS 3–4: Knit with color 1.

Rep these 4 rows until your motif is the desired size. BO after a Row 4.

(See page 129 for step-by-step instructions on knitted slip stitch.)

ASSEMBLY

As you complete the motifs, arrange them over the surface of your garment. Use the photos of our finished jackets for inspiration. Cont moving them around and rearranging them until you are pleased with the effect, making more motifs as needed.

Once you are satisfied, pin the motifs in place. Sew them directly to the garment. Add simple embroidery sts as desired to balance and complete your design. Weave in ends.

Should you wish you can work sc sts around the edges of the neck and sleeves, perhaps also adding a final row of crab st before embellishing your garment even further with a little creative needlework. Use yarn in the color of your choice and make simple sts in any arrangement you choose to create exciting embroidered detail. We embroidered simple lines in a starburst effect around our motifs.

Majestueux

Majestueux is the French word for majestic, which describes our richly colored jacket. The classic shaping is defined by slipped stitch motifs around the neck, front panels and bottom hem. In this project, we'll add more freehand embroidery and use crochet chain stitches on the surface to decorate around the motifs.

Level **2**

To make the jacket, work as for Level 1 (see page 83). If desired, add 2 additional skeins of yarn, each in a different color.

FREEFORM EMBELLISHMENTS

SLIP STITCH MOTIF (MAKE AS MANY AS DESIRED)

We hope you're enjoying making the slip st motifs, since this project will use even more of them. Experiment with different size motifs to add interest to your design. The finished patches can be either square or rectangular, but should be kept fairly small.

Work slip st motifs as for Level 1 (see page 83).

CROCHET CHAIN EMBELLISHMENT

Holding yarn at the back of the work, and the crochet hook at the front, pull through a loop of yarn at your starting point. Place the hook down though the knitting once again, at the position where you wish the next st to be. Wrap yarn around hook and pull the new loop through the knitting, plus, at the same time, through the loop on the hook. Cont adding sts in this manner until your design is complete. (See pages 118–119 for step-by-step instructions for crocheting through knitted fabric.)

ASSEMBLY

When you have a selection of motifs ready, lay them out on the surface of your garment and see how you like the effect. Add a few more, or take some away; adjust the sizes, or move the colors around. Our finished jacket is there to inspire you, but again it is only a guide—there are so many fabulous ways to use your motifs here. When you like what you see, pin the pieces in place and begin sewing them to your jacket.

Next, sc around the edges of the neck and sleeves. Stitch some whimsical embroidery around the knitted motifs to add interesting line and detail. Crochet ch sts through the knitting to link the embroidered stars.

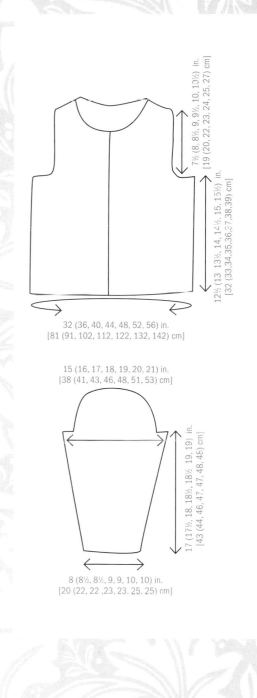

7½ (8, 8½, 9, 9½, 10, 10½) in.
[19 (20, 22, 23, 24, 25, 27) cm]

12½ (13, 13½, 14, 14½, 15, 15½) in.
[32 (33, 34, 35, 36, 37, 38, 39) cm]

32 (36, 40, 44, 48, 52, 56) in.
[81 (91, 102, 112, 122, 132, 142) cm]

15 (16, 17, 18, 19, 20, 21) in.
[38 (41, 43, 46, 48, 51, 53) cm]

17 (17½, 18, 18½, 18½, 19, 19) in.
[43 (44, 46, 47, 47, 48, 48) cm]

8 (8½, 8½, 9, 9, 10, 10) in.
[20 (22, 22, 23, 23, 25, 25) cm]

Phantasiereich

This long but fun name is the Portuguese word for imaginative. *Phantasiereich* takes our simple jacket design and adds a fantastic and imaginative collar to draw attention to our wonderful use of color, shapes and a great yarn! When we created this stylish jacket, we expanded on the techniques used for the slip stitch patches from *Levels 1* and *2* by adding a fun circular crochet motif. By now, your confidence in your own artistic abilities and your freeform experience will be your guide. We encourage you to think about your favorite stitches, motifs and techniques from other freeform projects, and consider adding them here. Are there other elements you would like to use in your *Phantasiereich* jacket? Then we say, go for it!

Level
3

To make the jacket, work as for Level 1 (see page 83). If desired, add 1 skein of yarn in each of 6 or more additional colors.

FREEFORM EMBELLISHMENTS

SLIP STITCH MOTIF (MAKE AS MANY AS DESIRED)

Work slip stitch motifs as for Level 1 (see page 83).

SMALL CROCHET CIRCLES (MAKE AS DESIRED)

We first explored crochet circle motifs with the fringed scarves on pages 27–33. Now let's make a few more slightly different circles, and blend them with our knitted slip stitch to make this collar a standout.

To begin the crochet circles, choose 2 colors. With color 1, ch 3, join with sl st to form a small ring.

RND 1: Ch 3, work 12 dc into ring. Cut color 1, join color 2.

RND 2: Ch 1, and work 2 sc into each dc of previous rnd. Fasten off.

ASSEMBLY

As you complete both the knit and crochet motifs, arrange them over the surface of your garment. Use the photos of our finished jackets for inspiration. Cont making more motifs, moving them around and rearranging them until you are pleased with the effect.

For the Level 3 garment, we didn't stitch the pieces directly onto the knitting. Instead, they were joined only to each other to create a separate collar that was eventually attached to the jacket at the neck and front edge.

This time, leave small spaces between the motifs as you arrange them, and then fill the gaps with random crochet. Filling these spaces with a web of openwork sts not only adds interest but also helps to keep your motifs securely in place. Any st or series of sts can be used to attach the motifs here. Don't worry about rows or order, just work intuitively to create your own unique weblike effect.

To complete the *Phantasiereich*, sew your completed collar into place around the neck edge. If you still want to keep playing with these wonderful colors and motifs, add more to your garment as you see fit. The bottom hem and cuffs are ripe with opportunity. Look for more ways to enhance your simple garment. Unleash with color and creativity!

Capes & Wraps

For this project, you'll try a new approach to freeform. Each of the capes and wraps in this section starts with a large felted rectangle of knit or crochet fabric. Then you'll cut these felted pieces into geometric shapes and connect them with freeform crochet stitches.

For these final three projects, our instructions are even more minimal than before, as you branch out on your own creative freeform journey. You are ready! Have fun with these last exciting projects. Remember all of the tips and suggestions we have already shared, listen to your own artistic muse and let your creative instincts guide you. Take our ideas and run with them (and, of course, you can always add even more ideas of your own as you see fit!). Make these projects uniquely you!

Project Basics

Basic information including the pattern for each level can be found with the rest of the level's instructions.

Extraordi-nariamente Mi

Extraordinariamente mi is a long way of saying uniquely me in Spanish. In this project, you'll cut a rectangle of felted fabric into a few random sections. Then add rows of freeform crochet directly to the edges of the felt. The crochet portion extends the top and bottom edges of the cut sections just a little...but the sides of the pieces extend much further outward, making the finished length of the reassembled rectangle almost twice as long as the original felted piece.

Level
1

FINISHED MEASUREMENTS

approx 18" × 70" (46cm × 178cm)

YARN

10 skeins SWTC Karaoke (Soysilk®/wool blend, 109 yds [100m] per 50g skein) (A)

1 skein SWTC Karaoke (Soysilk®/wool blend, 109 yds [100m] per 50g skein) in each of desired additional colors (8 skeins used in sample)

NEEDLES AND HOOKS

US size 8 (5mm) straight needles
size G (4mm) crochet hook
size B (2.25mm) crochet hook

NOTIONS

heavy paper for template
safety pins
yarn needle

GAUGE

18 sts and 24 rows = 4" (10cm) in St st, before felting

KNIT RECTANGLE

With yarn A, CO 180 sts. Work even in St st until piece measures approx 48" (122cm) from beg. BO.

FELTING

Felt knit piece to approx 36" (91cm) square. Lay flat and allow to dry completely. Using the heavy paper (taping sheets together as needed), create a template of finished wrap, approx 18" × 70" (46cm × 178cm). Cut felt into 4 or 5 random sections, arrange to roughly fill template, leaving a gap around each piece to fill with free-form crochet.

FREEFORM EMBELLISHMENTS

OUTLINING

Using the smaller crochet hook, outline each patch with a few crochet sts made as foll: Join yarn, *ch 2, skip the width of approx 2 sts, then work 1 sc into the felt, placing the hook approx

¼" (1cm) down into the fabric, and extending the first yarn-over upward until it reaches the edge of the felt before making the final yarn-over to complete the st. Rep from * around, fasten off. (See page 117 for step-by-step instructions on crocheting through felt fabric.)

Be sure to make sufficient sc sts and/or ch at any point where you are working around a corner so the sts are not stretched and the felt does not pucker. If you have cut your fabric using sweeping curves, you may also need to occasionally skip the ch sts altogether or work just 1 ch when crocheting into any dips in the fabric.

ADORNING

Once the initial rnd is complete, change to the larger hook and add further rows of crochet to the foundation row. Use taller sts such as dc, or vary the height of the sts as desired, creating bumps and bobbles as the mood takes you.

Hint: As with all freeform designs, watch the work carefully so you can be sure you are happy with the last few sts that have been made before moving on any further. And don't forget to place each piece onto the template periodically, to check that your additions are still on track to fit to your chosen pattern shape.

ASSEMBLY

Once you have added sufficient crochet sts and the pieces fit well within the boundaries of the pattern, crochet or hand stitch the sections tog to complete your wrap. Weave in ends.

Enveloppé
en Couleur

Wrap yourself in color with this mini-cape. Its French name translates as wrapped in color. Prudence has once again turned a simple felted piece into a spectacular garment with this dramatic capelet. Again you will cut into your felted piece, but this time you won't be cutting it into completely separate sections. In this design, a number of short cuts made around the neck edge on one long side of the felt allow you to overlap small sections of fabric and enable you to shape the garment so it falls gently from the shoulders. Deeper curved slashes along the other long edge frame inserts of freeform crochet that add drama and flair. Use our pictures as a loose guide to what you can accomplish as you create your own spectacular envelope of color.

Level
2

FINISHED MEASUREMENTS

approx 24" × 62" (61cm × 157cm)

YARN

14 skeins SWTC Karaoke (Soysilk®/wool blend, 109 yds [100m] per 50g skein) (A)
1 skein SWTC Karaoke (Soysilk®/wool blend, 109 yds [100m] per 50g skein) in each of desired additional colors (6 skeins used in sample)

NEEDLES AND HOOKS

US size 8 (5mm) straight needles
size G (4mm) crochet hook
size B (2.25mm) crochet hook

NOTIONS

safety pins
yarn needle

GAUGE

18 sts and 24 rows = 4" (10cm) in St st, before felting

KNIT RECTANGLE

With A, CO 136 sts. Work even in St st until piece measures approx 70" (178cm) from beg. BO.

FELTING

Felt knit piece to approx 20" × 58" (51cm × 147cm) square. Lay flat and allow to dry completely. Use a pin to mark the center point of the long top edge. Make 6 short cuts (approx 3" to 4" [8cm to 10cm] long) at approx 3" to 4" (8cm to 10cm) intervals from the pin (3 on each side of center). Place the fabric on 1 side of each cut over the top of the fabric on the other side of the cut, gently shaping the upper edge of the piece into a slight curve. Pin the overlapped fabric into place and sew tog. Next make approx 5 deeper cuts upwards from the lower edge. These cuts should be slightly wavy, rather than just straight slashes.

FREEFORM EMBELLISHMENTS

OUTLINING

Work as for Level 1 (see page 91), working in

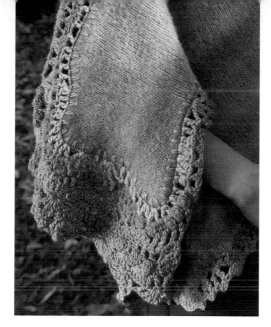

and out of the slashes all the way around the piece. (See page 117 for step-by-step instructions on crocheting through felt fabric.)

ADORNING

Once the initial rnd of crochet is complete, change to the larger hook and add additional rows of sts into the foundation row, filling the space between the slashes with interesting st combinations. Change yarns often, and randomly use different height sts, sometimes working them in groups and as clusters to create even more interest to the fabric as you fill in the gaps. Weave in ends.

Hint: When working the foundation row of crochet, carefully check after every few stitches to see how the work is progressing, so you can make sure you are adding the optimum number of stitches required. This is especially important when working around the curves and dips along the cut sections. Try the garment on often as you work the subsequent rows to ensure that the design flows in a pleasing manner.

Create any number of chain flowers as made for the Level 2 hat (see page 38), this time using the Karaoke yarn in your choice of color. (See page 113 for step-by-step instructions for chain flower.) Arrange them over the joins in the fabric around the neck, and scatter them anywhere you wish for added embellishment. Stitch neatly into position.

Libertad Artistica

We named our final garment using the Spanish expression for artistic freedom. All of the tips and techniques you have mastered as you worked through the many projects in this book have led you to this moment. *Libertad Artistica* is your final project and our final goal. You don't need a pattern now. This cape can be anything you want. It will grow from your own pattern pieces and can be shaped to fit your own fabulous figure. Have fun with this! Add colors that excite you and reflect your personality. Unleash your artistic freedom!

Level
3

FINISHED MEASUREMENTS

approx 72" × 55" (183cm × 140cm)

YARN

50 skeins SWTC Karaoke (Soysilk®/wool blend, 109 yds [100m] per 50g skein) in desired mix of colors (15 different colors used in sample)

NEEDLES AND HOOKS

US size 8 (5mm) straight needles
size G (4mm) crochet hook
size B (2.25mm) crochet hook

NOTIONS

safety pins
yarn needle
clasps
heavy paper for template

GAUGE

18 sts and 24 rows = 4" (10cm) in St st, before felting

KNIT SQUARES

With selected color, CO desired number of sts. Work even in St st until piece measures approx desired length from beg. BO. Rep until enough pieces have been knit to create the cape, allowing for shrinking after felting.

FELTING

Felt the knit pieces. Lay flat and allow to dry. Cut pieces into random shapes to create a patchwork look for the finished cape. Using heavy paper (taping sheets tog as needed), create a template for your cape design. (Alternately, use a commercial sewing patt for a cape.) Arrange pieces to roughly fill template, keeping pieces fairly near to the edges.

FREEFORM EMBELLISHMENTS

OUTLINING

Crochet around each piece as for Level 1 (see page 91), randomly using different colors as desired. (See page 117 for step-by-step instructions on crocheting through felt fabric.)

ASSEMBLY

Periodically spread out the paper patt and arrange all the motifs over it to get an idea of how many patches your garment requires, or how far the various areas of crochet mesh should extend from the felted centers. Resist the temptation to permanently join the motifs tog as they are completed, as you will generally be able to get a much better balance of all of the different shapes and colors if you leave the joining until you have sufficient pieces made to cover an entire section of patt. Small random shapes work well for filling in gaps between the patches, so create some additional crochet or knitted motifs in any size or shape you desire, and intersperse these among the patches.

SEAMING

Once most of the pieces are in place, add more rows of mesh sts and small random motifs to fill in any rem gaps in your design. Once you have everything arranged to your satisfaction, pin a few pieces tog at a time, and stitch them neatly. Then place this patch back into position on the template, and pin a few more pieces to each other. Joining the cape in sections will generally make it much easier to ensure that the completed garment retains the size and shape of the original patt. Leave slits for your hands, if desired (optional). Weave in ends. Sew clasps in place if desired.

Tip

I like to start by arranging my patches around the outside edges of the pattern template first, working my way inward toward the center of each pattern piece. Working in from the edge allows you to easily position the pieces with straightish edges along the front borders, or those with points along the lower edge where they will create a flowing and organic hemline.

Scarf Showcase

The International Freeform group on Yahoo! is home to thousands of amazingly talented freeform artists who share ideas, information and inspiration. We challenged several of our Freeform friends from this group by sending them each a bag of assorted SWTC yarns in a range of colors and asked them to create a scarf. We showcase their artwork here.

Notice how different each piece is. Many use the same stitches, techniques and yarns yet the results are dramatically different. It is why freeform is such a spectacular art form.

From the North Coast of New South Wales comes the creativity of **Lorraine Wiseman**. Lorraine and daughter Lisa create the most amazing garments—several of which are treasures in the SWTC collection.

Author and designer **Margaret Hubert** has been a friend and mentor to many of us. Here she showcases her work in signature style. As you become proficient in your freeform, your own style and flair will radiate. Prudence could identify Margaret's scarf from the group at a quick glance…and she was right!

Z. Phoenix shared some wonderful insight into her own love of freeform when she wrote, "I love free-form because it can be large or small, travel with me or stay home, express the concrete or the abstract, build from a sketched idea or, more often, spring from the moment and the materials, allowing me to be midwife instead of mother."

When I asked **Kathie Cureington** of Dothan, Alabama, why she loved freeform, her response was fantastic. She wrote, "I'm a gypsy; I've always been one and when I saw Prudence Mapstone's freeform crochet five years ago my fingers began to twitch and stitch, bullion's and scrumble's tumbled out... from Atlantic to Pacific...my heart hasn't stopped singing." We all echo her enthusiasm as artists.

Gwen Blakley Kinsler is a designer, author, and founder of the Crochet Guild of America. Her talent is showcased in her many books and patterns and on her website—www.crochetqueen.com.

Look carefully at the bottom of the left side of this scarf and you will notice the head of **Bonnie Prokopowicz's** signature doll with arms gracefully tucked at her side. Freeform surrounds the doll for a fabulous spin on this beautiful art.

Even as a child, **Diane Moyer** of Florida was never one to do a task exactly as told, always adding her own touch to it. Freeform allows her the freedom to play without rules and "just let it happen."

It's an honor to show the work of another avid free-former and lifeline artist, **Terri Lipman**. Terri used the rich colors of yarns and a lot of open lacework to create a light scarf that can be worn any time and anywhere.

Jorel Thomson is known for her bright and colorful work, so she was quite surprised when we challenged her with soft pastel colors. Jorel met the challenge head on, creating a trio of outstanding pieces that reflect her talent and style. In this lovely accessory, Jorel used open work, freeform lace to make a classic scarf.

Also from **Jorel Thomson**, we see more subtle tones and large freeform pieces used to create a smaller neck piece. The asymmetrical shaping made this an easy-to-wear and eye-catching piece.

This is the first freeform project that **Dodie Rush** of Pennsylvania has made. It was so exciting to see such a beautiful piece and learn about her inspiration. Inspired by the colors, she had fire and ice in mind as she set off on this freeform adventure.

Crochet Basics

When freeforming, you can often get away with many things that might be considered wrong in more traditional crochet. As we have pointed out before, we still want you to trust your instinct and let your own creativity shine through—but often it helps to understand the patterns before you start to change them. In the following pages, we outline the crochet techniques used in many of the patterns in this book.

If you have never crocheted before, this chapter will get you started. If you learned years ago but haven't crocheted recently, consider it a refresher course to help you brush up on your skills. Even if you have been crocheting steadily for years, you might still find that we mention a technique or two with which you are unfamiliar, so we hope that even the more experienced crocheters among you will use some of the explanations given toward the end of this chapter to expand your crochet repertoire.

Making a Slip Knot

Both the crochet and knit process generally begins with a slip knot, unless you are joining directly onto something that already exists. There are many different techniques for creating this initial stitch, some more complex than others. If you haven't tried it before, this simple version will get you started.

CREATE FIRST LOOP
Create a loop by bringing the short end of the yarn over the long end.

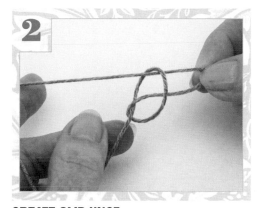

CREATE SLIP KNOT
Pull a loop from the long end through the loop you created in step 1 and tighten it up slightly.

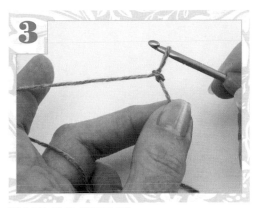

PLACE SLIP KNOT ON CROCHET HOOK
Place the loop on the crochet hook (or knitting needle) and pull it taut.

Creating a Chain

When working toward creating an initial freestanding row of crochet, the next step is to make a length of chain stitches into which the following row can be worked. This chain will be approximately the length of your first row. When making a crochet chain try to maintain an even tension, but be careful not to pull the loops too tightly once they are made. Remember that you will need to get your hook back into these loops again when you work the next row.

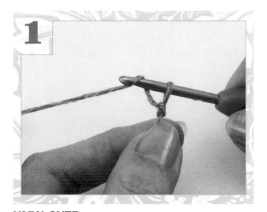

YARN OVER
After making the slip knot, yarn over by wrapping the yarn over the hook, from the back around to the front.

PULL YARN THROUGH LOOP
Pull the wrapped yarn through the slip knot to create the first loop.

CREATE CHAIN
Repeat steps 1 and 2 to create a second loop. Repeat until the chain is long enough. Count the slip knot as the first stitch in the chain.

Single Crochet

Illustrated below is one of the shortest crochet stitches. In the U.S. this stitch is called a single crochet stitch (abbreviated as sc), but in many other parts of the world (the U.K., Australia and some other English-speaking countries) it is known as the double crochet stitch (abbreviated as dc). This book uses US crochet terminology throughout the patterns.

Since single crochet stitches are short, the rows are fairly close together, so it will take quite a number of rows of these stitches to cover any given area. Consequently, a fabric worked entirely of single crochet stitches is generally quite firm and stable, unless you use a hook that is relatively large for the thickness of the yarn chosen.

SLIDE HOOK THROUGH FIRST CHAIN STITCH

After creating the chain, insert the hook from front to back into the second loop away from the hook.

YARN OVER

Make a yarn over by bringing the yarn from the back of the hook around to the front.

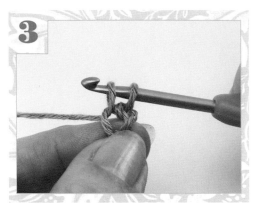

PULL YARN THROUGH LOOP

Pull the yarn through the chain stitch. There are now 2 loops on the hook.

YARN OVER

Wrap the yarn over the hook from the back to the front.

PULL YARN THROUGH BOTH LOOPS

Bring the yarn through the 2 loops on the hook. There is now 1 loop on the hook.

CONTINUE TO MAKE SINGLE CROCHET STITCHES

*Insert your hook into the next chain, and repeat steps 2 through 5 to make the next single crochet stitch. Repeat from * to continue making a row of single crochet stitches. At the end of this and every row chain 1 when turning for a new row. On subsequent rows, continue making single crochet stitches in the same manner, inserting your hook into a stitch from the row below each time you begin a new stitch.

Half-Double Crochet

The half-double crochet stitch is abbreviated as hdc. In the U.K., it is called the half-treble, and is abbreviated as htr. The half-double crochet stitch is a little taller than the single crochet stitch, but not as tall as the double crochet stitch that follows on the next page. Half-double crochet stitches are also slightly thicker than other crochet stitches because of the additional wrap that causes the yarn to travel through three loops on the hook at once. A fabric worked entirely with half-double crochet stitches is generally denser than one worked with either single or double crochet stitches.

YARN OVER

After creating the chain, make a yarn over by bringing the yarn from the back of the hook around to the front.

INSERT HOOK

Insert the hook, from the front toward the back, into the third chain from the hook.

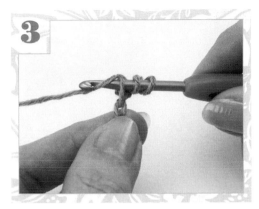

YARN OVER

Yarn over again by bringing the yarn from the back of the hook around to the front, and then draw this loop through the first loop only (3 loops now left on hook).

YARN OVER

Yarn over again by bringing the yarn from the back of the hook around to the front.

PULL YARN THROUGH NEXT 3 LOOPS

Draw the yarn through the 3 loops on the hook (1 loop now left on the hook).

CONTINUE TO MAKE HALF-DOUBLE CROCHET STITCHES

*Wrap the yarn again, Insert your hook into the next chain, and repeat steps 3 through 5. Repeat from *. At the end of this and every row, chain 2 when turning for a new row. On subsequent rows, continue making half-double crochet stitches in the same manner, inserting your hook into a stitch from the row below each time you begin a new stitch.

Double Crochet

The double crochet stitch (abbreviated as dc) is taller than both the sc and the hdc. In the U.K., it is called the treble, and is abbreviated as tr. A fabric made totally from double crochet stitches usually has more drape than one created in either single crochet or half-double crochet.

YARN OVER

After creating the chain, make a yarn over by bringing the yarn from the back of the hook around to the front.

INSERT HOOK

Insert the hook, from the front toward the back, into the fourth chain from the hook.

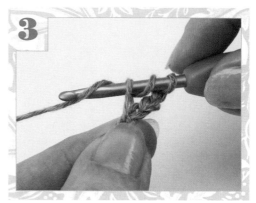

YARN OVER

Bring the yarn over the hook, from the back to the front.

PULL YARN THROUGH FIRST LOOP ON HOOK

Draw the yarn through the first loop on the hook (3 loops now left on the hook).

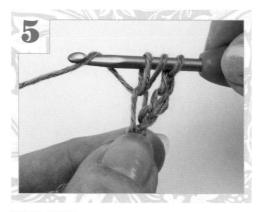

YARN OVER

Bring the yarn over the hook, from the back to the front.

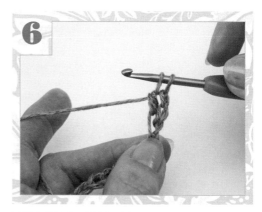

PULL YARN THROUGH NEXT 2 LOOPS

Draw the yarn through the first 2 loops (2 loops now left on the hook).

YARN OVER

Bring the yarn over the hook, from the back to the front.

PULL YARN THROUGH REMAINING LOOPS

Draw the yarn through the remaining 2 loops (1 loop now left on the hook).

CONTINUE TO MAKE DOUBLE CROCHET STITCHES

*Wrap the yarn again, insert your hook into the next chain, and repeat steps 3 through 8 to make the next double crochet stitch. Repeat from * to continue making a row of double crochet stitches. At the end of this and every row, chain 3 when turning for a new row. On subsequent rows, continue making double crochet stitches in the same manner, inserting your hook into a stitch from the row below each time you begin a new stitch.

Crocheting a Circle

Adding small crocheted circles to your freeform is a good way to avoid the angular look that sometimes develops in freeform, especially when joining many small square and rectangular knitted motifs together. Once you have mastered a few crochet basics, these circles are simple and quick to make.

BEGIN WITH A SMALL RING OF STITCHES
Chain 3, and join the stitches together with a slip stitch to form a small ring.

CHAIN 3 AGAIN
Chain 3 more stitches to bring your working yarn up to the height needed to begin the next stitch.

BEGIN TO FILL THE CIRCLE
Wrap the yarn around the hook and insert the hook into the ring. Bring the yarn over the hook and draw it through. Wrap the yarn over again, and draw it through the first 2 loops. Wrap the yarn over again, and draw it through the remaining 2 loops (i.e., 1 double crochet stitch made into the ring).

CONTINUE FILLING THE CIRCLE
Continue making more double crochet stitches into the ring, working until you have filled it with sufficient stitches to enable the motif to lie flat when joined (this usually takes approximately 11 or 12 double crochet stitches in all).

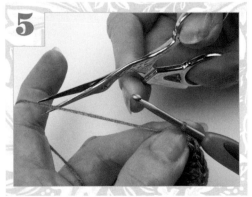

CLOSE THE CIRCLE, AND FINISH OFF
When you have worked sufficient double crochet stitches, slip stitch into the top of the 3 chain to close the circle, finish off and cut the yarn.

Crocheting an Open Circle

Open circles are an interesting variation to the preceding motif. You could begin by making a larger number of chains in the initial ring, but circles started in that manner are sometimes a little unstable. Wrapping the yarn a number of times around your finger helps pad the center, which results in a much firmer motif. For a smaller opening, wrap the yarn nearer to the tip of your finger or around a pencil; for a larger opening, try two fingers, your thumb or the wrong end of a large hook.

WRAP YARN AROUND FINGER
Wrap the end of the yarn around your finger a few times. The more times you wrap, the more padded the center of your circle will be.

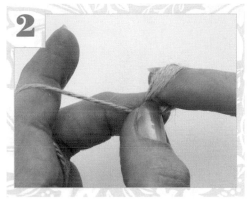

REMOVE WRAPPED YARN FROM FINGER
Grip the yarn between the thumb and one of the fingers on your other hand, and pull the circle of yarn off your finger.

BEGIN FIRST STITCH
Insert the hook into the center of the ring and make your first stitch. Single crochet stitches will make a small motif; double crochet stitches will make it larger. Using half-double crochet stitches will make a motif that is not only in between in size, but one that is also a little firmer and more stable than the other 2.

WORK AROUND CIRCLE
Continue creating more stitches until you have enough to fully fill the circle, and then join with a slip stitch and finish off.

Slip Stitch

A crochet slip stitch is basically a chain made after inserting the hook into another stitch. Slip stitches are often used for joining, as in the preceding circle motifs, and they can also be worked in rows. You may also use slip stitches to create a decorative border, as shown below.

CREATE FIRST LOOP
Create a loop by bringing the short end of the yarn over the long end.

MAKE FIRST SLIP STITCH
Insert the hook into the next stitch from the front toward the back. Wrap the yarn over the hook and pull the loop through the stitch and at the same time through the loop on the hook (1 loop now left on the hook).

CONTINUE SLIP STITCH
Repeat step 2 only to complete a row of slip stitches or to work slip stitches around the perimeter of any crocheted piece.

Creating Domes

These small crochet motifs will literally add another dimension to your freeforming. At the completion of the pattern, once the first and last stitches have been joined, the piece pops up to create a firm, circular, three-dimensional motif. This happens because the completed motif does not contain enough stitches to allow it to lie flat.

CREATE A SEMICIRCLE OF STITCHES
Chain 3 and join with a slip stitch to form a small ring. Chain 3 more, to get your yarn up to the height of the first stitch, and then work 5 or 6 double crochet stitches into the ring.

BEGIN JOIN
Insert the hook into the third of the 3 chain (i.e., the uppermost chain).

COMPLETE JOIN
Wrap the yarn around the hook, and draw the loop through the chain and also through the loop on the hook, to join and complete the motif. Finish off.

Creating a Bobble

Crochet bobbles are another easy way to help make your freeforming more tactile. The bobbles shown here can be made separately using a wide variety of different colors or even different yarns, and then tied into place.

Scatter them freely over the surface of your garments and accessories for additional interest and texture.

MAKE CHAIN
Begin by making a chain of 3 stitches.

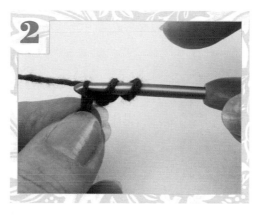

BEGIN STITCH
Wrap the yarn over the hook, and insert the hook into the slip knot.

PARTIALLY COMPLETE A DOUBLE CROCHET STITCH
Wrap the yarn over the hook and draw it through the slip knot, then wrap it over the hook again and draw it through the first 2 loops (2 loops now left on the hook).

MAKE MORE PARTIALLY COMPLETED DOUBLE CROCHET STITCHES
Repeat steps 2 and 3 three more times. Because you are not finishing off any of the double crochet stitches, you will be gaining an additional loop on the hook with each partially completed stitch. At the end of this step you will have 5 loops left on the hook. If you wish to make a larger bobble, repeat steps 2 and 3 a few more times (you gain 1 additional loop on the hook after every extra repeat).

COMPLETE THE BOBBLE
Wrap the yarn around the hook one last time, and draw it through all the loops on the hook. Finish off. Tie the completed bobble in place on one of your creations.

Creating a Corkscrew

Playful and interesting, corkscrews make a finished project fun. Discover for yourself how these little embellishments can add interesting details to purses, hats, or almost anything.

BEGIN INCREASES FOR CORKSCREW
Create a chain slightly longer than the desired length of the completed corkscrew. Insert the hook into the second chain from the hook, and work 3 single crochet stitches into this chain.

CONTINUE INCREASES
Continue making 3 single crochet stitches into the next and every chain following. After an inch (3cm) or so, the chain will begin to twist and will eventually spiral around. Continue making 3 single crochet stitches into each chain until you reach the end. Finish off. Larger corkscrews can easily be made by simply increasing the height of the stitches. More twisted corkscrews can be made by working more increases into each chain.

Creating a Leaf

Leaves add a beautiful, organic embellishment to any project. They're easy to make in both knit and crochet. The height of the stitches, in this instance worked along both sides of the foundation chain, dictates the shape of the crocheted leaves shown here.

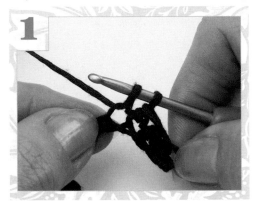

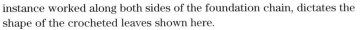

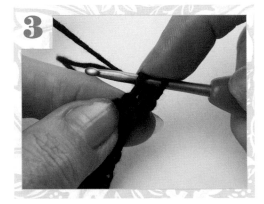

BEGIN LEAF
Chain the required number of stitches, as given in the pattern you're using. Insert the hook into the second chain from the hook, and begin working single crochet stitches into the chains, working the number specified in the pattern for the size of leaf you have chosen.

WORK THE INCREASES AND DECREASES
Continue working into the chain stitches as specified in the pattern, increasing the height of the stitches toward the center of the row, and then decreasing back down again by the end of the row.

CONTINUE BACK DOWN THE OTHER SIDE OF THE CHAIN
Do not turn the work over when you reach the end of the row, but instead chain 1 and then continue on, along the opposite side of the chain, again working the stitches in the order specified in the pattern. When completed, slip stitch to close, and finish off.

Creating a Starfish

These earthy little creations can also be the foundation for flowers. These little starfish are fast and fun to make. Use one color or many. Attach them evenly, or place them randomly around your project to create your own unique freeform effects.

CREATE CHAIN STARTING FROM CENTER AND BEGIN ARM

Chain 3 stitches and join with a slip stitch to form a small ring. Then chain 3 more stitches. Work 11 double crochet stitches into the ring, and join with a slip stitch to close.

Chain 7, insert the hook into the second chain from the hook and work 1 single crochet stitch into each of the next 2 ch.

INCREASE HEIGHT OF STITCHES

Work 1 half-double crochet stitch into each of the next 2 chains.

INCREASE HEIGHT EVEN MORE

Work 1 double crochet stitch into each of the next 2 chains.

CONNECT BACK INTO CENTER

Work 1 single crochet stitch into each of the next 2 stitches (note that the stitches you will now be working into will be double crochet stitches in the central circle). Continue on, following the starfish pattern as given in the pattern. If desired, finish off. If you wish to connect some of the starfish together as you make them, see the next steps described on page 112.

BEGIN TO CONNECT STARFISH

If you wish to connect starfish together, do so at the top of an arm. To begin a connecting arm, first repeat just the 7 chain from step 2.

CONNECT STARFISH

Before you continue back down the arm that you are going to connect, take the hook out of the last chain. Insert the hook into the top stitch on an arm on another completed motif, pick up the last chain again, and then proceed back toward the center of the motif as specified in the pattern.

Ruffled-Edge Flower

Make these fun flowers as frilly as you wish, just by increasing the number of stitches worked during the second round. Make them in a single color, or use two different shades. You might even like to consider adding a third round for an even more flamboyant flower, especially if your two-round flower is not as ruffled as you would like it to be. To give even more variety to your design, the additional round of stitches could be worked in single rather than double crochet stitches.

MAKE FLOWER CENTER AND BEGIN RUFFLED EDGE

Chain 3 and join with a slip stitch to form a small ring. Chain 3 more stitches, and then work approximately 15 or more double crochet stitches into the ring and slip stitch to close. If using 2 colors, finish off color 1 and join in color 2. Chain 3 and work 5 or 6 double crochet stitches into the first double crochet stitch in the previous round.

FINISH RUFFLED EDGE

Continue working 5 or 6 double crochet stitches into every stitch in the previous round. Increasing rapidly in this manner causes the edge of your flower to ruffle. Once you have worked all the way around the circle, slip stitch to close and finish off.

Chain Flower

This dainty little flower has been used on some of our felted hats (see page 38 and 39), where it was worked with a fine, sock-weight yarn. It looks just as good when worked in a thicker yarn, too, as we did on the *Level 2* cape (see pages 92 through 93). This motif can be attached with either the right or wrong side facing—the choice is yours.

MAKE FLOWER CENTER AND BEGIN FIRST PETAL LOOP

Chain 3 and join with a slip stitch to form a small ring. *Make approximately 5 more chains.

COMPLETE FIRST PETAL LOOP

Bend the chain over to form a large loop and slip stitch back into the ring. Repeat from * in step 1 plus step 2 four more times (a total of 5 petal loops made).

FILL PETALS WITH HALF-DOUBLE CROCHET

*Make sufficient half-double crochet stitches into the first petal loop to fill it well, and then make 1 slip stitch back into the ring. Repeat from * for each loop in turn, to fill all of the petals in the same manner. Finish off and attach the motif to your garment.

Crocheting a Ruffle

You have seen how increasing rapidly into each stitch in the previous round caused the outside round of stitches to ruffle in the flower (see page 112). In the same way, placing too many increases too close together in any other area also creates a similar ruffled effect. Follow the method described below to create a ruffle along the edge row of crochet stitches.

BEGIN RUFFLE

Join in yarn, and then chain to the height of your intended first stitch.

WORK INCREASES INTO SAME STITCH

Work 5 or more stitches into the next stitch. In this example we used double crochet stitches, but you could experiment with different stitches of different heights. The thinner the yarn, or the further apart the stitches you are working into, the more increases it will take to create a substantial ruffle.

CONTINUE WORKING INCREASES

Continue to work 5 or more stitches into each stitch. After 1 inch (3cm) or so the stitches should begin to ruffle well. If not, start making even more stitches into each stitch; or, if the piece begins to ruffle more than you wish, drop back to 1 or 2 fewer increases in each stitch. When you reach the end of the row, or when your ruffle is the desired length, finish off.

Creating Holes

Prudence intentionally made long, narrow holes in the work for added interest when she created the freeform belts for our bamboo skirts (see pages 74 through 79). Position your holes randomly along the length of your belt as often as you wish.

CHAIN OVER STITCHES TO CREATE HOLE

Follow the pattern for the belts until you come to the place where you wish to make a hole. Make a few chain stitches. Skip the same number of stitches in the row below, and then resume crocheting again as usual, until you come to the place where you wish to make the next hole.

WORK SINGLE CROCHET STITCHES IN CHAIN STITCHES

On the next row, when you reach a section of chain stitches, work a single crochet into each chain (or work the required number of stitches just into the large chain loop).

Crab Stitch (Right-Handed)

The crochet crab stitch is made in the same manner as the single crochet stitch, but it is worked in the opposite direction. Working in this manner twists the stitches, creating an interesting corded effect. When working crab stitch, right-handers crochet from left to right, while left-handers crochet from right to left. Crab stitch is traditionally used as an edging stitch, and it is demonstrated that way in the photos below.

BEGIN STITCH AS SINGLE CROCHET
With the right side of the work facing toward you, insert the hook into a stitch, wrap the yarn over the hook from the back toward the front, and draw the yarn through (the first stitch is just like a regular single crochet stitch).

INSERT HOOK INTO NEXT STITCH
From now on, you will be working in the opposite direction to normal. Insert the hook into the next stitch from front to back (i.e., a stitch to the right for right-handers and to the left for lefties).

YARN OVER
For many people, it is easier to remember how to do crab stitch if you learn to make the yarn over (just for this stitch) using a slightly different method. Place the hook above the working yarn, with the head of the hook facing down.

PULL LOOP THROUGH FIRST STITCH
Tilt the head of the hook downward, and scoop the yarn through the stitch you are working into, bringing it through to the front (to the left of the hook for right-handers, and to the right of the hook for lefties). Be careful not to slip through the loop already on the hook. There should now be 2 loops on the hook.

COMPLETE FIRST CRAB STITCH
Yarn over (in the normal fashion), and draw the yarn through the 2 loops on the hook (complete it as you would a single crochet stitch).

CONTINUE WORKING IN CRAB STITCH
Continue in this manner to complete a row of crab stitch. Normally a row of single crochet stitches are worked first, and the crab stitch is then worked into this foundation row. When freeforming though, you can work the crab stitch directly into the uneven edges of the fabric for a less regular, more organic row of stitches.

Crab Stitch (Left-Handed)

Even though right-handed people may think so, left-handed crocheters don't actually have an advantage when working this stitch since they, too, have to work it in the opposite direction to normal (from right to left). If you crochet with your left hand, you should follow the instructions given below, but also check out steps 3 and 4 on the right-handed version—the instructions for making a different style of yarn over. Whether you are left- or right-handed, placing the hook over the yarn and then scooping the yarn through in the manner shown better positions the head of your hook for tackling the next step, and seems to prevent a lot of crocheters from inadvertently creating a reverse slip stitch instead of the crab stitch.

BEGIN SINGLE CROCHET STITCH INTO EDGE

With the right side of the work facing toward you, insert the hook into a stitch, wrap the yarn over the hook from the back toward the front, and draw the yarn through (the first stitch is just like a regular single crochet stitch).

INSERT HOOK INTO NEXT STITCH AND YARN OVER

Follow the instructions for right-handed crab stitch steps 2 and 3, but work from right to left.

PULL LOOP THROUGH FIRST STITCH

Notice here how the stitches are moving from right to left.

COMPLETE FIRST CRAB STITCH

Yarn over and complete the stitch as you would a single crochet.

CONTINUE TO WORK IN CRAB STITCH

Follow steps 1 through 4 to continue working in crab stitch, working from right to left.

Crocheting Through Felt Fabric

When crocheting through felted fabric, a neat foundation row of stitches gives you an even base. Be sure your felt is firm around the edges, and work your stitches far enough down into the fabric to prevent the stitches from pulling out. Using a small sharp hook makes it easier to pierce the fabric. Be careful not to work your foundation stitches too tightly or too far apart, or the edge of the felt will buckle.

PUSH HOOK THROUGH FELT FABRIC

Push the crochet hook into the felt, from the front toward the back, creating a hole. You may need to wriggle the hook a little, especially if some areas of the felt are a little thicker than others.

CREATE FIRST ELONGATED STITCH

Yarn over and pull the yarn through the fabric, creating a loop on the hook. Pull this loop up loosely until it reaches to the edge of the fabric, and then yarn over and complete it as an elongated single crochet stitch.

PREPARE TO CROCHET AROUND CORNER

When your stitches are approaching a corner, make a hole and create a stitch just before you reach the corner.

CROCHET AROUND CORNER

Start another stitch in the same position by inserting the hook into the same hole as before, and then completing a second stitch. Continue working additional stitches into the same hole until you have rounded the corner sufficiently to move on to making a new hole. When working around sharply angled sections, be sure to stretch the elongated stitches far enough up so they do not compress the point.

Crocheting Through Knitted Fabric

A quick and easy way to embellish plain knitting is to work areas of crochet chain through the knitted fabric. The resulting crochet resembles embroidered chain stitch. Work fairly loosely as you make the crochet chains, and be sure that you do not stretch the stitches by placing them too far apart. Work geometric designs, or allow the stitches to travel randomly over the knitting by following a more instinctive path.

INSERT HOOK THROUGH FABRIC
Hold the yarn at the back of the knitted fabric, and the hook at the front. Insert the hook into the fabric, from the front toward the back, at the position you wish the first stitch to be. This does not necessarily need to be near an edge. Wrap the yarn over the hook from the back to the front.

PULL LOOP THROUGH FABRIC
Pull the yarn through to the front of the fabric, creating a loop on the hook. The working yarn will still be positioned at the back of the fabric.

INSERT HOOK AGAIN AND YARN OVER
Insert the hook back into the knitted fabric as before, and wrap the yarn over the hook again. Pull the yarn through the fabric and also through the loop that is on the hook.

CREATE ANOTHER STITCH
Repeat steps 1 through 3 to make the next chain stitch. Aim to work to an even tension that is neither too tight nor too loose to suit the drape of the fabric you are working into.

CONTINUE TO CHAIN STITCH
Continue making crochet chain stitches through the knitted fabric, following your chosen design.

SECURING CHAIN
When you have finished chain stitching your design, leave the last loop on the hook.

CUT YARN AND PULL THROUGH

Cut the yarn at the back of the work, and pull the tail end through to the front.

TUCK IN TAIL

Insert the hook through the fabric from the back to the front just slightly beyond the last stitch. Use the hook to catch the yarn tail and pull it through to the back. Weave the tail end neatly under a few of the chain stitch loops at the back of the work, and trim the yarn end as necessary.

Joining for a Reversible Motif

Two small separate pieces of fabric similar in size and shape can be held together and joined with a further round of crochet stitches. Because the resulting piece is reversible, it is ideal to use as fancy fringing, where either side of the completed motif could be on show at any time.

BEGIN FIRST JOINING STITCH
Crochet 2 circles, closing each with a sl st as they are completed. If joining them in the same color, leave the working yarn attached to 1 of the circles; if changing colors, finish both off completely, and join in another yarn. Hold the 2 motifs together with the wrong sides facing, insert the hook into one back loop from each circle, wrap the yarn around the hook and pull through.

CREATE A SINGLE CHAIN STITCH
Wrap the yarn around the hook and pull through to create a crochet chain stitch. Since in this instance we are joining circular motifs, from the next step onward we will need to make increases as we join.

BEGIN FIRST SINGLE CROCHET JOINING STITCH
Insert the hook into the back loops only of each next stitch on both motifs held together. Wrap the yarn around the hook, and bring the yarn through the 2 back loops.

TWO LOOPS ON HOOK
There will now be 2 loops left on the hook.

COMPLETE FIRST SINGLE CROCHET JOINING STITCH
Wrap the yarn around the hook, and draw it through these 2 loops to complete a single crochet joining stitch. Work another single crochet joining stitch into the same 2 back loops.

WORK MORE JOINING STITCHES
Move onto the next stitch, and repeat steps 3 to 5, continuing until you join right around the entire edge. Once the round of joining sts is complete, slip stitch into the first chain stitch to connect the first and last stitches, but do not finish off if you intend to use this motif for a fringe.

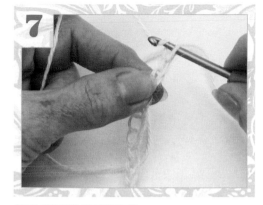

ADD CHAIN STITCHES

When using this type of double-sided motif for a fringe, add chain stitches to approximately double the length desired for the finished fringe.

ADD OTHER STITCHES TO END OF CHAIN

Once the length of chain stitches is the desired length, turn and work a corkscrew (see page 110) into the first few chain stitches. The more chain stitches you work into, the longer the corkscrew will be.

Connecting Fringe

Simple lengths of crochet fringe have been used to full effect on the skirts (see pages 74 through 79) and purses (see pages 46 through 51) we created for this book. Rather than make each length separately, which would make the joining process very time consuming, join a few lengths of fringe together as you go to create small bunches of fringe.

BEGIN TO CREATE SIMPLE FRINGE

Make a length of crochet chain approximately as long you wish the completed section of fringe to be.

MAKE FRINGE THICKER

Turn, miss the first chain and work a row of single crochet stitches. If you wish to have a wider fringe, miss the first 3 chains after the turn and work in double crochet. For perfectly straight fringe, work to the same tension as your chain stitches. For slightly twisted fringe, work with a tighter or looser tension than for the chain.

CONTINUE TO MAKE FRINGE

When you reach the end of a row, start a new chain and begin to join another length of fringe to the bunch. Once enough small bunches of fringe have been completed, arrange them onto your finished items in a freeform manner, and tie or neatly stitch into position.

Attaching Fringe

Double-ended fringes, as shown on pages 120 to 121, can easily be attached to your garments without any additional stitchery. Secure each fringe simply by looping it through the edge of the piece.

PULL FRINGE THROUGH FABRIC

Fold a section of the chain stitches over, a little off center. Pull the folded loop through the crochet or knit fabric. If the fabric is loosely constructed, you will be able to do this with your fingers, but if the stitches are firm and tight it will be easier to use a crochet hook.

SECURE FRINGE

Drop the tail ends of the fringe through the chain loop, and pull to tighten the loop and secure the fringe in place.

Knitting Basics

We've provided some simple knitting techniques and explanations to help you with our patterns. If you need more guidance with knitting, we recommend finding a yarn store nearby and taking a class or two. It won't take long to get you ready to tackle the basic patterns in our book. We've kept them all simple so that the real creativity is in the exploration of color and embellishment.

Long-Tail Cast On

The long-tail cast on is a long-time favorite. It produces a clean, stretchy edge perfect for Stockinette stitch or ribbing. Remember to cast on loosely to make it easier to work the first row of stitches.

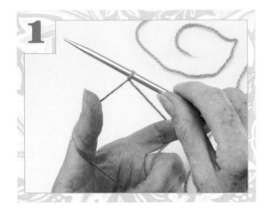

MAKE A SLIP KNOT
Make a slip knot (see page 101), leaving a long tail. One rule of thumb suggests leaving approximately 1" (3cm) for every stitch you'll be casting on plus 12" (30cm). Slide the slip knot onto a knitting needle. Tighten the loop. Hold the needle in your right hand and grab the tail and working yarn with your other hand. Create a triangle, with the tail wrapped around your thumb and the working yarn wrapped around your index finger. Secure the yarn with the remaining fingers of the same hand to create the proper tension.

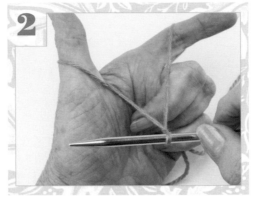

POSITION YARN
Pull the needle down, forming a v with the yarn.

SLIP NEEDLE UNDER YARN ON THUMB
Bring the needle under the yarn on your thumb.

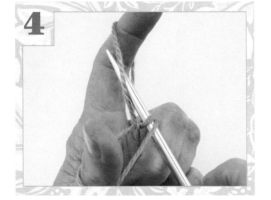

BRING NEEDLE OVER YARN ON INDEX FINGER
Bring the needle over the yarn on the index finger, grabbing it with the needle tip.

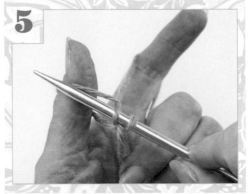

PULL YARN THROUGH LOOP ON THUMB
Pull the yarn through the loop formed by the thumb, creating a new stitch.

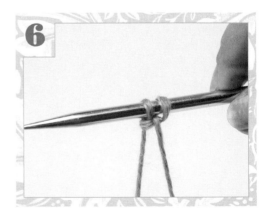

TIGHTEN LOOP
Release your thumb and forefinger and pull the loop taut. Repeat the process as many times as needed.

Cable Cast On

The cable cast on is a flexible and slightly stretchy method of casting on. After creating a slip knot and the first cast-on stitch, subsequent stitches are created by placing the needle between the two previous stitches. Making stitches in this manner prevents the stitches in the cast-on row from twisting, and places them in the correct position for knitting the first row.

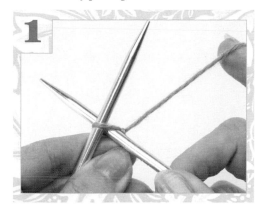

1 MAKE SLIP KNOT AND BEGIN
Make a slip knot on the left-hand needle (see page 101). Holding the yarn to the back, insert the right-hand needle through the slip knot from front to back.

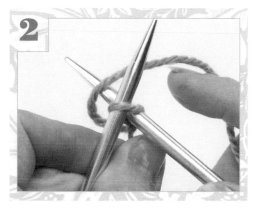

2 WRAP YARN
Wrap the yarn around the point of the right-hand needle as shown.

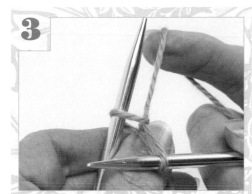

3 BRING YARN THROUGH LOOP
Pull the right-hand needle through the slip knot, catching the wrapped yarn and creating a new stitch.

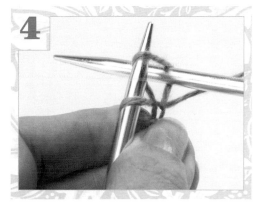

4 SLIDE NEW STITCH ONTO LEFT-HAND NEEDLE
Slide the new stitch onto the left-hand needle.

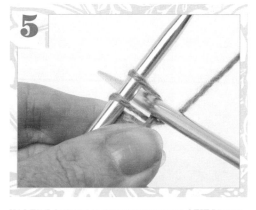

5 INSERT NEEDLE BETWEEN THE STITCHES
Insert the right-hand needle between the 2 stitches on the left-hand needle from front to back.

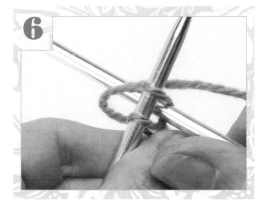

6 WRAP YARN
Repeat step 2, wrapping the yarn around the tip of the left-hand needle as before.

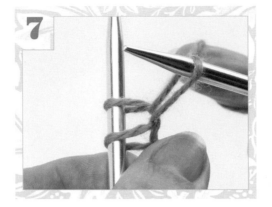

BRING YARN THROUGH LOOP

Pull the right-hand needle through, catching the wrapped yarn and creating a new stitch.

SLIDE NEW STITCH ONTO LEFT-HAND NEEDLE

Slide the new stitch onto the left-hand needle. Repeat steps 6 and 7 to cast on the number of stitches specified in the pattern.

Knitting

The knitting method shown here is often referred to as the throwing technique. This is because the yarn is "thrown" (or wrapped) around the right-hand needle before the stitch is pulled through. When using this method, the yarn is held in the right hand. The working yarn remains behind the needles as you create the stitches. At first you may find you need to take this hand off the needle to complete step 2, but with a little practice it is possible to speed up your knitting by throwing the yarn without letting go of the right-hand needle.

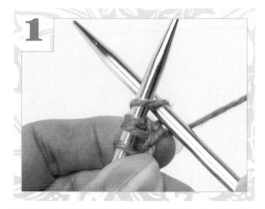

INSERT NEEDLE THROUGH FIRST STITCH

Insert the right-hand needle into the first stitch on the left-hand needle from front to back. The right-hand needle should cross behind the left-hand needle.

WRAP YARN OVER RIGHT-HAND NEEDLE

Wrap the working yarn around the right-hand needle as shown.

CREATE NEW STITCH

Dip the tip of the right-hand needle down to pull the wrapped yarn through the stitch on the left-hand needle and bring the yarn up on the right-hand needle, creating a new stitch and allowing the old stitch to drop off the left-hand needle. The new stitch remains on the right-hand needle.

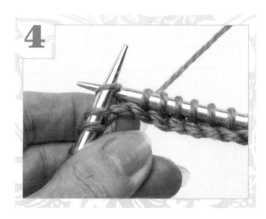

CONTINUE KNITTING

Repeat steps 1 through 3 to continue knitting.

Purling

The purling method shown here is also done using the throwing technique. Your yarn will remain in the right hand. The working yarn remains to the front of the needle as you create the stitches. Again, after a little practice you should be able to complete the stitch without taking your hand off the right-hand needle.

INSERT NEEDLE THROUGH FIRST STITCH

Slide the tip of the right-hand needle into the front of next stitch to be worked on the left-hand needle, from top to bottom. The right-hand needle should cross in front of the left-hand needle.

WRAP YARN OVER RIGHT-HAND NEEDLE

Wrap the working yarn around the tip of the right-hand needle as shown.

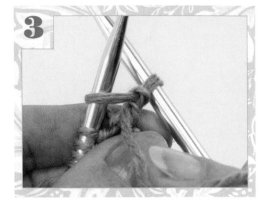

DRAW YARN THROUGH STITCH

Draw the right-hand needle back through the stitch, catching the wrapped working yarn with the tip of the needle and bringing it back through the stitch on the left-hand needle.

DROP OFF OLD STITCH

Allow the old stitch to drop off the left-hand needle, creating a new purl stitch on the right-hand needle.

CONTINUE PURLING

Repeat steps 1 through 4 to continue purling across the row.

Knitted Slip Stitch

A two-color knitted slip stitch pattern is a great way to add more color to your freeform knitting. Prudence has added them to the jackets on pages 80 through 87. Slip-stitch knitting as used in these motifs involves slipping some of the stitches of one color up over 2 rows, and then working the following two rows in plain knitting with the other color. For a 1 × 1 slip-stitch pattern, such as in the motifs we have used for embellishment in our open jackets, you should always begin by casting on an odd number of stitches.

KNIT FIRST STITCH, SLIP SECOND STITCH

To begin, cast on the desired number of stitches using Color 1, and knit 1 row (this row will be on the wrong side). Join in Color 2. This next row will be Pattern Row 1 from page 83, and will be the right side of the motif. Knit the first stitch with Color 2 (orange) and slip the second stitch of the other color (purple).

KNIT NEXT STITCH, SLIP STITCH AFTER

Continue knitting and slipping stitches in this manner, right across the row. Then continue to follow the pattern for the knitted slip stitch motif given on page 83 (the next row you work will be Pattern Row 2). Continue following the 4 row motif pattern (the following 2 rows will be plain knitting using Color 1), until your motif is the desired size.

Knitting I-Cord

I-cord is a simple type of tubular knitting that can come in handy in many ways. Use it as we did, for fancy fringes, or sew it onto a piece of fabric to outline some of your motifs. Thread it through knitted eyelets or open-mesh crochet stitches. Twist it up and stitch it to the surface to embellish plain areas, or attach it to edges to create button loops. The possibilities for freeforming with I-cord are endless. Always use double-pointed needles, since you will be sliding the stitches to the other end of the needle and working each next row without turning.

BRING WORKING YARN TO BEGINNING OF ROW

Cast on a small number of stitches (2–4 stitches work best). In this example, there are 3 stitches. Without turning the needle or moving the stitches in any way, bring the working yarn across the 3 stitches and knit the first stitch as usual.

FINISH FIRST ROW

Knit across all 3 stitches as usual.

CONTINUE KNITTING I-CORD

Again, bring the working yarn behind the stitches to the beginning of the row. Do not turn the work or move the stitches. Continue working in this manner until the I-cord is the desired length, then slip the first stitch, knit the next 2 stitches together, and pass the slipped stitch over to finish off.

Increasing and Decreasing

Even before you start the freeform embellishments, you will need to know how to increase and decrease stitches so you can shape many of the basic patterns. You will also use the same technique to vary the shape of some of the random motifs, such as when making the knitted border or leaves for the *Basic Tees* project (see pages 66 through 73). The photos below show how to make a simple increase or decrease. They are worked here at the beginning of a row of knitting, as you might work them when knitting a leaf motif.

BEGIN INCREASE

To make an increase, insert the right-hand needle into the stitch, wrap the yarn over and draw it through the loop, but do not yet complete the stitch.

COMPLETE INCREASE

Take the point of the right-hand needle around behind the left-hand needle, insert it into the back of the loop still on the left-hand needle, and knit the stitch again, before dropping the old stitch off the needle.

BEGIN DECREASE

To make a decrease, insert the right-hand needle from front to back through 2 stitches at once, just as for knitting a single stitch (i.e. right-hand needle will go into the second stitch on the left-hand needle before the first stitch).

COMPLETE DECREASE

Wrap the yarn around the needle and draw it through both loops at once to make 2 stitches become 1.

Binding Off

Once any section of knitting reaches the size specified in the pattern (or if working randomly, the desired size), you will need to bind the stitches off as you remove them from the needles to permanently secure them. The simple method shown below involves lifting stitches, one over the other one at a time, and creates a firm, neat edge. When binding off, be sure you do not inadvertently tighten your tension, as a bind-off row worked to a firmer gauge will cause the work to pull inward.

KNIT TWO STITCHES
Knit the first 2 stitches in the row just as you would for a normal knitted row.

INSERT LEFT-HAND NEEDLE INTO FIRST STITCH
Insert the left-hand needle into the first knitted stitch on the right-hand needle.

PASS FIRST STITCH OVER SECOND STITCH
Pass the first stitch over the second knitted stitch.

DROP FIRST STITCH OFF NEEDLE
Allow the first stitch to drop off the needle. There is now 1 stitch on the right-hand needle.

CONTINUE BINDING OFF
Knit the next stitch on the left-hand needle and then repeat steps 2 through 4 to bind off the remaining stitches.

SECURE END
When 1 stitch remains on the right-hand needle, cut the yarn and pull the tail through the stitch. Pull the yarn taut to secure the bind-off row, then weave in the end.

Three-Needle Bind Off

The three-needle bind off is another technique for finishing off your knitting. It allows you to bind off two pieces of fabric together and create a beautiful, seamless join between them. This technique is especially useful for a nice finish on shoulders!

HOLD BOTH SECTIONS TOGETHER

Hold the 2 sections of knitting together, with the right sides facing toward each other. You should have the same number of stitches on each needle.

INSERT NEEDLE

Take a third needle of the same size, and insert it though the first stitch on both sections of knitting.

WRAP YARN

Wrap the yarn around the new needle to begin a knit stitch, just as when creating a regular knit stitch.

DRAW LOOP THROUGH

Draw the loop through both stitches at once to complete the knit stitch and drop both loops off the left-hand needle.

PASS FIRST STITCH OVER THE SECOND STITCH

Make another knit stitch in the same manner by working into the next 2 stitches on the left-hand needles at the same time. Use the point on 1 of the left-hand needles to pass the first stitch on the right-hand needle over the second stitch on the right-hand needle.

CONTINUE 3-NEEDLE BIND OFF

Repeat step 5 until the bind-off row is complete. Finish off and weave in end. You can see how this bind-off technique creates a seamless, smooth join.

Mattress Stitch

Mattress (also known as ladder) stitch is a neat and flexible way to join two sections of knitting or crochet. It leaves only a small ridge at the back of the work when seaming the sides of knitted pieces to each other, and is also a great seaming technique for attaching freeform areas to each other. Done properly, it has more stretch than a back-stitch seam, and so it does not constrain the fabric, and when worked into the sides of the stitches on the edges of freeform patches, it makes a flexible and virtually invisible join.

THREAD YARN AND BEGIN
Thread either the tail end of the working yarn or a new piece of yarn onto a blunt-ended yarn (or darning) needle. If using a new piece of yarn, make a couple of back stitches on the wrong side of the work to secure. Insert the needle into 2 loops (legs of the stitch) on the right side of the seam. The further in these loops are, the larger the ridge it will make at the back.

TAKE YARN TO OTHER SIDE OF JOIN
Take the needle across to the other piece of fabric, and insert it into 2 loops on the left side of the seam.

LOOSELY MAKE LADDER, THEN TIGHTEN
Continue crossing back and forth in this manner, working your stitches loosely to create a ladder effect. Make 6 to 8 stitches in this way, and then gently pull the yarn taut to close the seam.

PUT EASE INTO THE SEAM
Place your fingers on either side of the fabric at the spot just before these last stitches began, and use the other hand to gently pull on the seam to add ease. Continue in this manner, each time working 6 to 8 loose stitches before tightening and adding ease, until your seam is completed.

Resources and Information

Basic Knitting and Crochet Information

Standard Knitting and Crochet Abbreviations

beg	beginning
C5F	cable 5 front
CC	contrast color
ch(s)	chain
cn	cable needle
dec	decrease
dpn(s)	double-pointed needle(s)
foll	following
inc	increase
k	knit
KFB	knit 1 front and back
k2tog	knit 2 together
k3tog	knit 3 together
LLI	left lifted increase
M1	make one
MC	main color
p	purl
(in) patt	(in pattern)
pm	place marker
p2tog	purl 2 together
p3tog	purl 3 together
psso	pass slipped stitch over
rem	remaining
RLI	right lifted increase
RS	right side
rep	repeat
SKP	slip 1, knit 1, pass slipped stitch over
SK2P	slip 1, knit 2 together, pass slipped stitch over
sl	slip
SSK	slip, slip, knit
st(s)	stitch(es)
work 2 tog	work 2 together
WS	wrong side
w&t	wrap and turn
wyib	with yarn in back
wyif	with yarn in front
yo	yarn over

Knitting Needle Conversions

diameter (mm)	U.S. size	suggested yarn weight
2	0	Lace Weight
2.25	1	Lace and Fingering Weight
2.75	2	Lace and Fingering Weight
3.25	3	Fingering and Sport Weight
3.5	4	Fingering and Sport Weight
3.75	5	DK and Sport Weight
4	6	DK, Sport and Aran/Worsted Weight
4.5	7	Aran/Worsted Weight
5	8	Aran/Worsted and Heavy Worsted
5.5	9	Aran/Worsted, Heavy Worsted and Chunky/Bulky
6	10	Chunky/Bulky
6.5	10½	Chunky/Bulky and Super Bulky
8	11	Chunky/Bulky and Super Bulky
9	13	Super Bulky
10	15	Super Bulky
12.75	17	Super Bulky
15	19	Super Bulky

Crochet Hook Conversions

diameter (mm)	U.S. size	suggested yarn weight
2.25	B-1	Lace Weight
2.75	C-2	Lace and Fingering Weight
3.25	D-3	Lace and Fingering Weight
3.5	E-4	Fingering and Sport Weight
3.75	F-5	DK and Sport Weight
4	G-6	DK, Sport and Aran/Worsted Weight
4.5	7	Aran/Worsted Weight
5	H-8	Aran/Worsted and Heavy Worsted
5.5	I-9	Aran/Worsted, Heavy Worsted and Chunky/Bulky
6	J-10	Chunky/Bulky
6.5	K-10½	Chunky/Bulky and Super Bulky
8	L-11	Chunky/Bulky and Super Bulky
9	M/N-13	Super Bulky
10	N/P-15	Super Bulky
15	P/Q	Super Bulky
16	Q	Super Bulky
19	S	Super Bulky

Yarn Weight Guidelines

Since the names given to different weights of yarn can vary widely depending on the country of origin or the yarn manufacturer's preference, the Craft Yarn Council of America has put together a standard yarn weight system to impose a bit of order on the sometimes unruly yarn labels. Look for a picture of a skein of yarn with a number 1–6 on most kinds of yarn to figure out its "official" weight. Gauge is given over Stockinette stitch. The information in the chart below is taken from www.yarnstandards.com. The great thing about freeform is that gauge and yarn weight don't matter so much. Just play until you get it right.

Substituting Yarns

Freeform just begs for yarn substitution! Use whatever you have in your stash, no matter the weight or material. However, if you are following a pattern to make a base garment, choose a yarn and needle/hook combination that achieves the proper gauge. If not, you may end up with a misshapen thing that you won't want to wear. Also consider substituting a yarn with a similar fiber content to the one recommended in the pattern so you'll get a similar effect and drape to what you see in the pictures.

	Super Bulky (6)	Bulky (5)	Medium (4)	Light (3)	Fine (2)	Superfine (1)	Lace (0)
Type	bulky, roving	chunky, craft, rug	worsted, afghan, aran	dk, light worsted	sport, baby	sock, fingering, baby	fingering, 10-count crochet thread
Knit Gauge Range	6–11 sts	12–15 sts	16–20 sts	21–24 sts	23–26 sts	27–32 sts	33–40 sts
Recommended Needle in U.S. Size Range	11 and larger	9 to 11	7 to 9	5 to 7	3 to 5	1 to 3	000 to 1

Special Knitting Techniques Glossary

BINDING OFF

Binding off refers to securing stitches, generally at the edge of a knitted garment or motif. The most basic method of binding off is to knit two stitches, then slip the first knit stitch over the second and off the needle. This process is repeated until all the stitches are bound off, or secured. In addition to this method, there are many other ways of binding off. Follow the method specified in the pattern for the best result.

THREE-NEEDLE BIND OFF

A three-needle bind off works well for joining live stitches. This bind off is generally used when two pieces of knitting with the same number of stitches need to be seamed together, such as shoulder seams or the toes of socks. The "live" stitches for both pieces are kept on separate needles and lined up exactly, stitch for stitch. A third needle is used to work the bind off, by inserting it through the first pair of stitches together, knitting them together, knitting the second pair of stitches together and then sliding the first knit stitch over the second and off the needle. Just as for the traditional bind off, this process is repeated until all the stitches have been bound off.

CASTING ON

Casting on refers to creating the number of stitches needed for the first row of any project. There are several methods for casting on. In most cases, you may use the method with which you are most comfortable. However, when a specific cast on is indicated in the pattern, it's best to follow that method since the designer most certainly used it for a good reason.

BACKWARD-LOOP CAST ON

This simple cast-on method is often used to add stitches in the middle of a knitted piece as opposed to casting on stitches for the very beginning of a piece. (For example, you might use this method to cast on stitches for a buttonhole.) To cast on with the backward-loop method, simply use your fingers to make a loop in the working yarn, making sure the yarn crosses the base of the loop on the left. Simply slip this loop onto the needle and pull it snug. Repeat to cast on the number of stitches as indicated.

CABLE CAST ON

Make a slip knot and slide it onto the left-hand needle. Holding the yarn to the back of the work, insert the right-hand needle through the slip knot, from the front towards the back. *Wrap the yarn around the point of the right-hand needle, bringing it around from the back toward the front. Bring the point of the right-hand needle through the slip knot, catching the wrapped yarn to create a new stitch. Slip the new stitch onto the left-hand needle. Insert the right-hand needle between the 2 stitches on the left-hand needle, from the front toward the back. Repeat from * until you have the number of stitches specified in the pattern, or if working randomly, the number desired.

LONG-TAIL CAST ON

Leaving a long tail (approximately ½" to 1" [1cm to 3cm] for each stitch to be cast on), make a slip knot and slide it onto the right-hand needle so the tail falls in front of the needle and the working yarn falls behind it. Insert your thumb and index finger between the yarn ends so the working yarn is around your index finger and the tail end is around your thumb. Maintain tension on the triangle you created by holding the ends with your other fingers. Turn your palm upward to make a V with the yarn. *Bring the needle in front of the loop on your thumb, grabbing it with the needle. Bring the needle over the strand around your index finger, pulling the resulting stitch through the loop on your thumb. Drop the loop off your thumb, and placing your thumb back into the V configuration, tighten the resulting stitch on the needle. Repeat from * for the number of stitches indicated.

DECREASES

Practically speaking, decreases reduce the number of stitches on the needles. They can also become integrated into the design when worked symmetrically, row after row, to create darts or visible lines of any other type.

KNIT TWO TOGETHER (K2TOG)

This decrease is the simplest of all. To create a right-leaning decrease, slip the right-hand needle through the first two stitches on the left-hand needle from front to back, as for a regular knit stitch. Knit the two stitches as one. To knit three together (k3tog), perform the same operation with three stitches instead of two.

SLIP, SLIP, KNIT (SSK)

This decrease slants to the left. Slip the first stitch as if to knit, slip the second stitch as if to knit, then insert the left needle into the fronts of both stitches and knit them together.

I-CORD

To make I-cord, cast on a small number of stitches, three or four works best, to one DPN. Knit one row. Slide the stitches to the opposite end of the needle without turning the work. * Pulling the yarn across the back, knit one row. Slide the stitches to the opposite end of the needle, again without turning the work. Repeat from *, creating a tube. When you reach the desired length, break the yarn, pulling it tight through all the stitches. Weave the end of the yarn back through the tube. Sew the end of the I-cord to an earflap or mitten cuff to make a handy tie. Or graft the I-cord to knitted fabric with mattress stitch as a decorative element.

INCREASES

Some increases lean to the right, and others to the left. When increases are spread out evenly over several rows, it doesn't really matter which way they slant. However, increases aligned row after row are quite noticeable and become attractive design elements.

Following are some of the most commonly paired increases.

KNIT ONE FRONT AND BACK (KFB)

An easy way to increase is to knit one in the front and back of a stitch (KFB). To make this type of increase, simply insert your right-hand needle into the next stitch on the left-hand needle and knit the stitch, keeping the stitch on the left-hand needle instead of sliding it off. Then bring your right-hand needle around to the back, knit into the back loop of the same stitch, and slip both stitches off the needle.

MAKE ONE (M1)

This right-leaning increase is made by inserting the tip of the right needle from front to back into the bar between the next stitch and the stitch just knit. Place this loop onto the left needle and knit into the back of it.

PICKING UP STITCHES

To pick up a stitch, insert the tip of one needle through the side of a stitch from front to back. Leaving about a 3" to 4" (8cm to 10cm) tail, wrap the yarn around the needle as you would for a regular knit stitch. Bring the yarn through the stitch, creating a loop on your needle. This loop is the first picked-up stitch. Continue to pick up the number of stitches required, making sure to space them evenly.

PLACING (AND SLIPPING) A MARKER (PM AND SM)

Sometimes a pattern calls for you to place a marker (pm) and slip a marker (sm). Markers are generally small plastic rings that slide onto a needle and rest in between stitches, marking a certain spot. If you don't have markers on hand, cut small pieces of scrap yarn in a contrasting color. Tie the scrap yarn around the needle in the indicated spot in a loose knot. Move the marker from one needle to the other when you come to it. Continue as usual.

SEAMING

Two main methods are used to seam knitted pieces together in this book. *Mattress stitch* is used to seam pieces with bound-off edges together, or to seam pieces together along their sides. *Kitchener stitch* is used to graft two rows of live stitches together. Both methods create a seamless join from the right side, and Kitchener stitch is seamless from both the front and back of the work.

KITCHENER STITCH

To graft with Kitchener stitch, line up both sets of live stitches on two separate needles with the tips facing the same direction. Thread a yarn needle onto the tail of the back piece. Begin by performing the following steps once: Bring the yarn needle through the first stitch on the needle closest to you as if to purl, leaving the stitch on the needle. Then insert the yarn needle through the first stitch on the back needle as if to knit, leaving the stitch on the needle. Now you are ready to graft. * Bring the yarn needle through the first stitch on the front needle as if to knit, slipping the stitch off the needle. Bring the yarn needle through the next stitch on the front needle as if to purl, leaving the stitch on the needle. Then bring the yarn needle through the first stitch on the back needle as if to purl, sliding the stitch off the needle. Bring the yarn needle through the next stitch on the back needle, leaving the stitch on the needle. Rep from * until all the stitches are grafted together. Approximately every 2" (5cm), tighten up the stitches, starting at the beginning of the join. Slip the tip of the yarn needle under each leg of each Kitchener stitch and pull up gently until the tension is correct. Repeat across the entire row of grafted stitches. It may help you to say to yourself, "Knit, purl—purl, knit" as you go.

MATTRESS STITCH

You'll work mattress stitch differently depending on whether you are seaming vertically or horizontally. For both vertical-to-vertical and horizontal-to-horizontal seaming, you'll begin the same way. Place the blocked pieces side-by-side with right sides facing. With yarn needle and yarn, insert the needle from back to front through the lowest corner stitch of one piece, then in the lowest corner stitch of the opposite piece, pulling the yarn tight to join the two pieces.

To work vertical-to-vertical mattress stitch, work back and forth as follows: On the first piece, pull the edge stitch away from the second stitch to reveal a horizontal bar. Insert the needle under the bar and pull through. Insert the needle under the parallel bar on the opposite piece and pull through. Continue in this manner, pulling the yarn tight every few rows. Weave the end into the wrong side of the fabric.

To work horizontal-to-horizontal mattress stitch, work back and forth as follows: With bound-off stitches lined up stitch for stitch, insert the needle under the first stitch inside the bound-off edge to one side and pull it through, then under the parallel stitch on the other side and pull it through. Continue in this manner, pulling the yarn tight every few rows. Weave the end into the wrong side of the fabric.

A Word About Felting

There is no exact formula for felting with any traditional fiber, and the same is true even when using a more unusual combination, such as the SWTC Karaoke Soysilk®-and-wool blend yarn. Your gauge, knitting style and even water will affect how much the project felts during washing. Your own preference (softly felted or thoroughly felted) will also determine the yarn you'll choose.

Determining the Shrinkage Factor

You will need to make your own adjustments to the size of the knitted piece, depending on the size of the finished garment you want to make. To calculate the size of the piece you will need to knit before felting, we recommend that you first make and felt a good size swatch, before you begin work on the larger piece. You can always use this swatch as the foundation for a fancy freeform hot pad. Once you are a freeformer, nothing need ever be wasted.

Make and measure your finished swatch and write down the needle size, and how many stitches and how many rows you worked to make it. Run the swatch through the wash in the same way you plan to felt the larger piece until the swatch is felted to your satisfaction. Calculate the percentage of shrinkage, and then calculate the number of stitches you will need to make a large enough piece of felt for your project. Because you will be adding random crochet to bring the felted pieces up to the final required size, it isn't a major problem if the larger piece ends up felting slightly more (or less) than the swatch, or even if your calculations are not absolutely exact.

Felting SWTC Karaoke

SWTC Karaoke yarn is a blend of Soysilk® and wool. It does not felt exactly like wool. To felt it, toss your knit piece into your laundry. It will shed excess fiber, so a pillowcase or fine washable bag is highly recommended. Or just wash it by itself. In its first time through your wash, it will full, or lightly felt, with some of the stitches often still visible. If you like the soft hand and halo, leave it like this. If you desire a firmer fabric, repeat the process. The more times through the wash, the stiffer and more obviously felted the fabric will become.

Some Advice About Felting

What if your piece doesn't felt right? The problem we see most often with felting is that the knit piece was treated too gently in the washer. Get rough with it! Add a pair of jeans or tennis shoes to this load and a little soap (but no bleach!). Use the hot wash and hot rinse cycle. If the piece still doesn't look felted enough, a second round through will usually do the trick.

When you are happy, lay it out to dry, tugging it into shape if necessary.

There's a lot of fiber in my wash from the felting! Yes...that's why we recommend using a fine washable bag or pillowcase when putting knit pieces into your laundry to felt. It will shed and leave behind some fiber. Please don't forget this step!

Resources

Visit your local yarn store, craft store or online vendor to buy yarn, knitting needles, crochet hooks and other notions. Here are a few of our favorite suppliers, and online educational and inspirational sites.

60 ODD, A FIBER ODYSSEY

www.60odd.50webs.com
An online exhibition featuring 60+ freeform crochet artworks.

THE CROCHET GUILD OF AMERICA

http://crochet.org
The Crochet Guild of America is a not-for-profit educational organization dedicated to preserving and advancing the art of crochet, and is a rich resource for crochet fans worldwide. Known also as CGOA, the guild hosts magnificent national and regional conferences, publishes a crochet magazine, and encourages education and mentoring.

INTERNATIONAL FREE FORM CROCHET GUILD

http://groups.yahoo.com/group/FFCrochet
Discussion group where you can share information, ideas, techniques and photos, or ask questions regarding freeform style crocheting.

INTERNATIONAL FREEFORM FIBERARTS GUILD

www.intff.org
Check out two inspiring online freeform exhibitions from 2007 here, including Earth, Wind, Air and Fire, Water and Tree of Life/Tree of Peace.

THE KNITTING GUILD ASSOCIATION

www.tkga.com
Like the crochet guild, the Knitting Guild Association (TKGA) provides knitters with educational resources, including their well known certification program that offers credentials useful for those interested in design, teaching or just furthering their own skills.

KNOT JUST KNITTING

www.notjustknitting.com
Prudence's website is a complete freeform experience. Let the Gallery photos showcasing her creations inspire you. You will also find additional instructions, patterns and ideas (plus details of Prudence's other books and tutorials) to help you on your freeforming journey.

RAVELRY

www.ravelry.com
The largest international social networking site for knitting, crochet and the fiber arts.

SYLVIA COSH AND JAMES WALTERS' FREEFORM CROCHET SITE

http://crochet.nu
U.K. creative crochet pioneers—this site is a celebration of scrumbling and all creative crochet styles

CLOVER

www.clover-usa.com
Clover provided us with their wonderful crochet hooks to use in our projects. From traditional bamboo hooks to their new Soft Touch Hooks, Clover is a world leader in crochet hooks and accessories.

SIGNATURE NEEDLE ARTS

www.signatureneedlearts.com
Signature Needles will become your favorites. These spectacular handcrafted, made-in-the-USA needles are special. Each needle is a gorgeous work of art that makes your knitting glide in your hands. These are heirloom accessories and well worth the investment.

SOUTHWEST TRADING COMPANY, INC. (SWTC INC)

www.SOYSILK.com
This company pioneered earth friendly yarns and fiber and continues to lead the industry with new, cutting-edge yarns. They first introduced SOYSILK® brand fiber, bamboo, and corn fiber and continue to excite. Keep an eye on SWTC, where creativity is a lifestyle. Visit the website for a list of independent yarn stores that carry this yarn.

Index

Check out these other knitting and crochet books for more patterns and inspiration

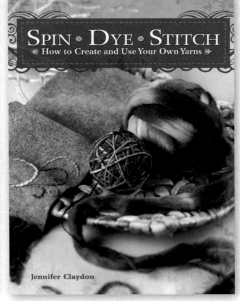

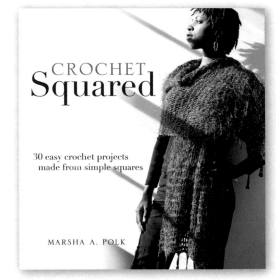

Socks a la Carte
by Jonelle Raffino

Flip through the split pages of this book and knit up some fancy footwear. Choose from sock heels, toes and bodies to design your perfect socks. With thousands of possibilities, you're sure to find the perfect sock for you. A helpful techniques section in the front of the book teaches you all the basics of sock knitting.

ISBN-13: 978-1-60061-185-8
ISBN-10: 1-60061-185-0
hardcover, 128 pages, Z2729

Spin Dye Stitch
by Jennifer Claydon

Learn the basic techniques of making and using beautiful handspun yarns. *Spin Dye Stitch* takes you through the entire process—from fiber to finished garment. Jennifer Claydon's simple, clear instructions show you how to make yarn by drop spindling and wheel spinning, as well as how to dye fibers safely and simply before or after spinning. Whether you're a knitter, crocheter, weaver, embroiderer or complete newcomer to the fiber arts, you're sure to love *Spin Dye Stitch*.

ISBN-13: 978-1-60061-155-1
ISBN-10: 1-60061-155-9
paperback, 128 pages, Z2490

Crochet Squared
by Marsha Polk

If you can crochet a simple scarf, you can make any of the stylish and sophisticated body wraps and accessories featured in **Crochet Squared**. Each of the over 20 projects in the book is based on a simple square or rectangle shape, allowing even beginning crocheters to make gorgeous works of art.

ISBN-13: 978-1-58180-833-9
ISBN-10: 1-58180-833-X
paperback, 128 pages, 33507